ENGLISH DRAMATISTS

Series Editor:
Bruce King

ENGLISH DRAMATISTS
Series Editor: Bruce King

Published titles

Susan Bassnett, *Shakespeare: The Elizabethan Plays*
Richard Allen Cave, *Ben Jonson*
Philip McGuire, *Shakespeare: The Jacobean Plays*
Kathleen E. McLuskie, *Dekker and Heywood*
Christine Richardson and Jackie Johnston, *Medieval Drama*
Roger Sales, *Christopher Marlowe*
David Thomas, *William Congreve*
Martin White, *Middleton and Tourneur*
Katharine Worth, *Sheridan and Goldsmith*

Forthcoming titles

John Bull, *Vanbrugh and Farquhar*
Barbara Kachur, *Etherege and Wycherley*
Maximillian Novak, *Fielding and Gay*
Rowland Wymer, *Webster and Ford*

ENGLISH DRAMATISTS

DEKKER AND HEYWOOD

PROFESSIONAL DRAMATISTS

Kathleen E. McLuskie

Pro-Vice Chancellor, University of Kent

St. Martin's Press

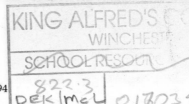
© Kathleen E. McLuskie 1994

First published in Great Britain 1994 by
THE MACMILLAN PRESS LTD
Houndmills, Basingstoke, Hampshire RG21 2XS
and London
Companies and representatives
throughout the world

A catalogue record for this book is available
from the British Library.

ISBN 0-333-46236-X hardcover
ISBN 0-333-46237-8 paperback

Printed in Hong Kong

First published in the United States of America 1994 by
Scholarly and Reference Division,
ST. MARTIN'S PRESS, INC.,
175 Fifth Avenue,
New York, N.Y. 10010

ISBN 0-312-10629-7

Library of Congress Cataloging-in-Publication Data
McLuskie, Kathleen.
Dekker and Heywood / by Kathleen E. McLuskie.
p.   cm. — (English dramatists)
Includes bibliographical references (p.   ).
ISBN 0-312-10629-7
1. Dekker, Thomas, ca.1572–1632—Criticism and interpretation.
2. Heywood, Thomas, d.1641—Criticism and interpretation.
3. English drama—17th century–History and criticism.   4. London
(England)—Popular culture—17th century.   5. Theater—England–
–London—History—17th century.   I. Title.   II. Series: English
dramatists (St. Martin's Press)
PR2494.M35   1994
822' .3—dc20   93–30472
                                                   CIP

Contents

Editor's Preface

Each generation needs to be introduced to the culture and great works of the past and to reinterpret them in its own ways. This series re-examines the important English dramatists of earlier centuries in the light of new information, new interests and new attitudes. The books are written for students, theatre-goers and general readers who want an up-to-date view of the plays and dramatists, with emphasis on drama as theatre and on stage, social and political history. Attention is given to what is known about performance, acting styles, changing interpretations, the stages and theatres of the time and theatre economics. The books will be relevant to those interested in or studying literature, theatre and cultural history.

BRUCE KING

Acknowledgements

My thanks to all my friends and colleagues who made this book possible. Richard Proudfoot kindly let me see the typescript of his Malone Society edition of *Tom O' Lincoln*, the 'Women, Text and History' seminar at Oxford made helpful comments on the section on women. The librarians at the University of Kent searched for material, sent for inter-library loans and were tolerant of my tardiness in returning books on Dekker and Heywood. Jean Howard and Phyllis Rackin listened to the arguments with their accustomed learned enthusiasm. Andrew Butcher, Rod Edmond, Tom Healy, Marion O'Connor, Jonathan Sawday and Sue Wiseman helped in a variety of ways. As always, the greatest debt for tolerance and time is to David Turley and Anna, Hilary and Celia.

1
Fireworks All Over the House

I

In the preface to the reader, affixed to the 1613 edition of *The White Devil*, John Webster praised Chapman, Jonson, Beaumont and Fletcher and 'lastly (without wrong last to be named) the right happy and copious industry of Master Shakespeare, Master Dekker and Master Heywood'.[1] In linking the names of Shakespeare, Dekker and Heywood, Webster was referring to playwrights associated with the three most important companies then working in London: the King's Men at the Globe and Blackfriars, Prince Henry's Men at the Fortune theatre, and Queen Anne's Men at the Red Bull, the theatre in which Webster's play was first performed. Dekker's and Heywood's critical fortunes have not equalled those of their illustrious fellow[2] but, like him, they were professionals, and it is as professionals that their work offers a useful vantage point from which to understand the conditions of theatre as it became firmly established in the artistic and commercial world of London at the turn of the seventeenth century.

The concept of the professional writer was both new and highly contested.[3] However, it usefully describes the activity of those dramatists who were employed on a regular basis by major companies. They worked on their craft, drawing on available raw material in collections of narratives and other plays, and were able to turn their hands, as occasion required, to dramatising a contemporary scandal or adding a few scenes to the revival of an old play.[4]

Dekker and Heywood wrote for the whole range of London theatres from the down-market amphitheatre, the Red Bull in the north of the city, to the club-like intimacy of the theatre within St Paul's Cathedral. Their plays were also seen at court and the dedications to the printed versions suggest at least some measure of gentry and aristocratic patronage.[5] However, their principle and primary relationship to their art was one dominated by the marketplace. As well as histories, comedies and tragedies, Dekker and Heywood produced professional theatre versions of court masques, topical plays responding rapidly to current affairs and verses which provide the scripts for the elaborate shows with which the City's guilds welcomed the Lord Mayor into London. They engaged, in other words, with all the opportunities available for professional dramatists in the new, commercial theatre world of early modern London. As such, their work can provide an insight into the cultural movement in which literary arts began to be transformed into the commodities of a consumer economy which at the same time enacted and articulated the beliefs and aspirations of the society which produced and consumed them.

The record of Heywood's career in the theatre begins in the autumn of 1596 when Henslowe, the theatrical entrepreneur who funded the Admiral's Men, recorded 30 shillings 'lent unto them for hawodes bocke'. In 1598 he was hired to Henslowe 'as a covenante searvante for ii yeares . . . not to playe any wher publicke a bowt london . . . but in my howsse'. [6] His subsequent career as sharer and principal playwright for Worcester's Men and, after 1603, for the Queen's Men, put him at the centre of London's commercial theatre world. Dekker's career as a playwright was a more journeyman affair. He frequently appears in Henslowe's records as a part of a team of play-producers[7] as well as producing in 1599, his best-known play, *The Shoemaker's Holiday* for the Admiral's Men. Dekker's free-floating career brought him fewer financial rewards (he was in prison for debt from 1614–18)[8] than those provided by the joint professions of actor, shareholder and playwright enjoyed by Heywood and Shakespeare. His work illustrates the eclecticism of a professional career which followed the shifting commercial opportunities, crossing the boundaries between élite and popular theatre venues and companies, and collaborating with, among others, Webster, Middleton and Ford.[9]

The formal, artistic and political challenges offered by the dramatists' movement among different venues and companies is the subject of the remainder of this book. What needs emphasis here is the extent to which Dekker and Heywood were involved in a larger shift in the culture of their time. As Andrew Gurr has shown,[10] the establishment of a permanent commercial theatre in London involved considerable amounts of investment, and fundamentally altered relations between audience and playwrights. The need for a steady stream of new plays increased the opportunities which a career in playwriting offered the young man of letters, but a return on that investment required a more extended audience. These changes caused anxieties and opportunities which were extensively commented on by contemporaries as players and writers, readers and theatre audiences came to terms with the changes in their situation as producers and consumers of culture. Dekker and Heywood were extremely self-conscious about their roles in a changing theatrical scene. In the prefaces and dedications to their plays, they recognised their dependence on patronage, and yet they acknowledged the actors as providing them with access to an audience and making them part of a new market in leisure.

Their attitudes to this fundamental cultural change were as ambivalent and contradictory as the social relations that underpinned it. Both writers joined in the vigorous debates about the stage but the voices in their polemic were always in disguise, playing with the genre and form of the works in which it appears, negotiating the relationship with the audience and the market for different forms of writing. In the address to the reader of *The Wonderful Year*, Dekker presents the players as ingratiating hacks, careless of the value of the works they perform. He entreated his audience 'as Players do in a cogging Epilogue at the end of a filthy Comedy that, be it never such wicked stuffe, they would forbeare to hiss'.[11] However, elsewhere Dekker offered a full and generous appreciation of the role of the players in fostering the arts of poetry and learning. Dedicating *If This Be Not a Good Play the Devil is in It* 'To my Loving, and Loved Friends and Fellowes the Queenes Maiesties Seruants' he asserted that

> I haue cast mine eye upon many, but find none more fit, none more worthy, to *Patronize* this, than you, who haue *Protected* it. Your Cost, Counsell, and Labour, had bin ill spent, if a *Second* should by my hand snatch from you *This Glory*.   (17–21)[12]

Dekker's most extended analysis of the new theatrical situation comes in *The Gull's Hornbook* where he offers a clear sense of the commercial realities of the theatre:

> The theatre is your poets' Royal Exchange upon which their Muses – that are now turned to merchants – meeting, barter away that light commodity of words for a lighter ware than words – plaudits. . . . Players are their factors who put away the stuff and make the best of it they possibly can. . . .Your gallant, your courtier and your captain had wont to be the soundest paymasters . . . when your groundling and gallery commoner buys his sport by the penny and like a haggler is glad to utter it again by retailing.

Dekker's description suggests that, by the early years of the seventeenth century, the theatre and the market have become one: poets provide the commodity which is dealt in by the players and purchased by the audience; patronage has become a matter of commerce and the principal patrons the paying audience. This change, in Dekker's view, had a profound effect on the relations between the players and their audience. He observed that the theatre

> is so free in entertainment, allowing a stool as well to the farmer's son as to your Templar, that your stinkard has the self same liberty to be there in his tobacco fumes which your sweet courtier hath.[13]

The new relationship with the audience was contested, in Dekker's *Satiromastix*, a hybrid play, whose triple plot offered a

romantic narrative of 'murdered honour', a witty comedy of a
widow's remarriage and at the same time engaged in a lively
exchange with the great apologist for high art, Ben Jonson. In
Poetaster, to which *Satiromastix* was a reply, Jonson had satirised
Dekker as 'Demetrius Fannius' a dresser of plays, associated
with the down-market trade of players, dependent for patronage
on commercial relations with the *nouveaux riches*. At the end of
the play, he makes Demetrius Fannius admit that his opposition
to Jonson was no more than envy:

> no great cause . . . I must confesse: but that hee kept better
> company (for the most part) than I: and that better men lov'd
> him, than lov'd me: and that his writings thriv'd better than
> mine and were better lik't and grac't: nothing else.
>
> (V, iii, 449–53)[14]

Dekker responded by mocking Jonson's pretentious delusion
that aristocratic patronage could put him above the need to
co-operate with the players who performed his plays. In
Satiromastix, he makes the figure of Jonson/Horace promise that
he will not

> sit in a Gallery, when your Comedies and Enterludes have
> entred their Actions, and there make vile and bad faces at
> euerie lyne, to make Sentlemen haue an eye to you, and to
> make Players afraide to take your part. (V, ii, 298–301)

Dekker's complex account of the shifting relations between
the poet and the players may have been an aspect of his rather
precarious hold on a theatrical career. Heywood, on the other
hand, was more confident about his firm connection to the
theatrical profession. He dedicated his *Apology for Actors* to 'My
good Friends and Fellowes the Citty Actors' and placed his
polemic above the fray of the contemporary anti-theatrical
controversy by stressing the theatre's antiquity. In doing so, he
presents the theatrical profession with a confident view of its
own cultural significance, placing it in the long tradition of
classical and European theatre. He included a celebration of the
great actors of the previous age, Tarleton, Kemp and Edward

Alleyn, which argued for actors' high social and moral status.
But he also made clear his concern to rid the theatre of abuses:

> I also could wish that such as are condemned for licen-
> tiousness, might by a generall consent bee quite excluded our
> society; for, as we are men that stand in the broad eye of the
> world, so should our manners, gestures, and behaviours,
> savour of such government and modesty to deserve the good
> thoughts and reports of all men.[15]

In insisting on the theatre's social and moral status, Heywood
was rejecting the earlier jibe that actors were simply masterless
men, dependent on the favours of a rootless commercial audience. He attempted to draw to actors the cultural importance of
other writers in furthering agreed moral and political aims. He
quotes Cicero's advice to Caesar that players would busy the
people 'which otherwise be inquisitive after thee and thy greatness' but he also stresses the general didactic function of drama:

> Art thou inclined to lust? behold the falles of the Tarquins in
> the rape of Lucrece; the guerdon of luxury in the death of
> Sardanapalus; Appius destroyed in the ravishing of Virginia,
> and the destruction of Troy in the lust of Helen. . . .
>   We present men with the uglinesse of their vices to make
> them more to abhorre them. (Sig. G)

He thus refutes the charges that the theatre as a medium of
popular entertainment had sustained in earlier attacks, without
acknowledging them.

In its insistence on the theatre's moral power, *An Apology for
Actors* merely rehearsed commonplaces of Renaissance criticism.
However, it is also, like Dekker's *Gull's Hornbook*, constantly
negotiating its relationship with the new context for theatre.
Unlike many of those who had written in defence of theatre,
Dekker and Heywood stood in a professional rather than a
pedagogic or pastoral relation to their audience and were
accordingly, more prepared to allow them to take responsibility
for their response:

Players are in use as they are understood
Spectators eyes may make them bad or good
(p. 51)

In insisting on the appeal of theatre for both princes and 'any bold English man', and in acknowledging the right of those who could pay to judge the performance, Dekker and Heywood were signalling their desire to please the widest possible market.

In the new artistic and commercial situation, however, the dramatists had a unique opportunity to create that appeal as well as satisfy it. The market for their art was far from unified or homogeneous. Dekker's partiality for the Queen's Men in the dedication of *If This Be Not a Good Play the Devil is in It* was in contrast to his attitude to his former employers, the Prince's Men at the Fortune. He appreciated their support for his work because

When *Fortune* (in her blinde pride) set her foote upon *This imperfect Building,* (as scorning the *Foundation* and *Workmanship:*) you, gently raizd it up. . . .To you therefore deseruedly is the Whole Frame consecrated. (ll. 21–5)

Dekker's appreciation of the players' role was not matched by confidence that the new audience could be trusted to judge art. He begins the prologue to *If This Be Not a Good Play the Devil is in It,* by suggesting

Would t'were a Custome that at all New-playes
The Makers sat o'th Stage, either with *Bayes*
To haue their *Workes Crownd,* or beaten in with *Hissing.*
(1–3)

This sounds similar to his attack on Jonson in *Satiromastix,* but later in the same prologue he denounces the popular audience with a bitterness worthy of Jonson himself:

A Play whose *Rudenes, Indians* would abhorre,
Ift fill a house with Fishwiues, *Rare, They All Roare.*
It is not praise is sought for (Now) but Pence,

Tho dropd, from Greasie-apron *Audience*.

(17–20)

It seems ironic that Dekker should denounce a low-life audience in a prologue performed at the most notoriously popular theatre venue, the Red Bull. However such terms as 'Greasie Apron' or 'Fishwives' did not only denote specific social groups but were used as cultural counters in an effort to locate and relocate the boundaries between high and low culture. For Dekker the highest aim of the poet was to

> draw with *Adamantine Pen*, *(euen creatures*
> *Forg'de out of th'Hammer*,) on tiptoe, to *reach*-up,
> And (from *Rare silence*) clap their *Brawny hands*,
> *T'Applaud*, what their *charmed* soule scarce understands.

(33–6)

In asserting art's educative function, its capacity to refine as well as please a popular audience, Dekker was claiming a role as an intellectual guardian of taste, offering it across the boundary of élite and popular culture to those who are so often simply rejected as incapable of understanding.

In the context of twentieth-century culture, Andrew Ross has shown how popular culture has always to be defined in opposition to an élite alternative. Those definitions are the province of

> experts in culture, whose traditional business is to define what is popular and what is legitimate, who patrol the ever shifting borders of popular and legitimate taste, who supervise the passports, the temporary visas, the cultural identities, the threatening 'alien' elements, and the deportation orders, and who occasionally make their own adventurist forays across the border.[16]

Those borders were beginning to be established at the turn of the seventeenth century and discussions about the art and purpose of playing involved conflict among those who aspired to be the guard-patrol.

Modern efforts to understand the debate over élite and popular culture in the seventeenth century are vitiated by the terms of the debate which still continues today. The art of the past is one of the strongest weapons in the modern debate with the result that the cultural politics of a professionalised education system are conducted with the outdated weaponry of an earlier conflict. Modern discussions of 'popular' dramaturgy in the Renaissance move variously between analysis of the audience, to discussion of the subject-matter of the plays, to the forms of the drama itself, in which the residual native traditions of liturgical and morality plays are seen as more inherently 'popular' because of the way they directly acknowledge their physical relationship with the audience.[17] In focusing on cultural politics and the aesthetic judgements attendant upon them, they too often bypass the theatrical and artistic necessities which determined the shape and form of the plays. One route out of this confusion is to substitute the term 'professional' for the more culturally-loaded concept of the popular. To consider Dekker and Heywood as 'professional' dramatists, insists instead on relations with particular companies and conditions of production and has as its model of creativity a set of theatrical resources, from court shows, from classical learning and from the native traditions of theatre which lay behind the performers' skills and which the dramatists deployed to make plays for them.

II

At the heart of the professional dramatists' relationship to their plays lay the question of form. They dealt in a drama in which, at least in the early years, the variety of theatrical pleasures offered seemed more significant than coherence of plot or theme, or the subtle development of character. The title-page advertisement for Heywood's *Edward IV*, for example, offered a double plot and multiple ancillary actions; it appealed as much to variety as to principles of artistic cohesion:

> The first and second parts of King Edward the fourth containing his merry passtime with the Tanner of Tamworth, as also his loue to faire Mistresse Shore, her great promotion, fall and miserie, and lastlie the lamentable death of both her and her husband. Likewise the beseiging of London, by the

bastard Falconbridge, and the valiant defence of the same by
the lord Maior and Citizens.[18]

Each of these plots would be enough for a full-length play if they
dwelt on cause and effect, character, motive and action.
However, here the treatment is episodic, plots are initiated and
almost completed before being dropped in favour of the next
action. Nonetheless, the achievement of this plotting should not
be underestimated for as the action of Part II draws to a close,
figures and episodes long forgotten emerge with a telling effect
on the outcome. The two parts seem to have been planned as a
whole, with the planting of episodes whose significance will
appear only in the final unfolding of the whole plan.

This emphasis on variety as the central pleasure of theatre is
equally evident in Dekker's *Old Fortunatus* which transforms folk
material and magic to create theatrical form. The source for the
play was a German *Volksbuch* whose first part, like Dekker's first
and second acts, deals with the adventures of Fortunatus, and
the second part presents the story of his sons. The *Volksbuch*
included all the plot-elements of a magic hat (to travel all over
the world) and a magic never-empty purse. There were also
magic apples which could bring horns out on sinful heads and
take them away again, and a princess spirited away by the very
resourceful hero who is plotted against by her vengeful suitors.
As Cyrus Hoy suggests, 'It will be readily acknowledged that
there is sufficient material in this rambling narrative not only for
a two- but for a three- or even four- part play.'[19] Dekker's extant
play reworked an earlier version to which a second part was
added and the play then further adapted for court performance.
This process of adaptation and reworking lay behind Jonson's
jibes at Dekker as a 'dresser of plays'. However, Dekker's role
also indicates the possibility of a different conception of the
dramatist's art. The variety of episodes offer different opportunities for theatrical 'turns' and are loosely held together by a
chorus which, as the prologue explains, meet the demands of
narrative.

> And for this smal Circumference must stand
> For the imagind Sur-face of much land,
> Of many kingdones, and since many a mile,

Should here be measurd out: our muse intreats,
Your thoughts to helpe poore Art, and to allow,
That I may serve as Chorus to her scenes,
She begs your pardon, for sheele send me foorth,
Not when the lawes of Poesy doe call,
But as the storie needes.

                                        (Prologue, 15–23)

The pleasures of this kind of theatre lie in the discrete
theatrical elements of a variety of set pieces. The play opens with
a comic monologue from Fortunatus 'meanely attired . . .
cracking nuts' in which his every speech is mocked by an Echo
and is followed by the allegorical set piece of Fortunatus's
dream, of Fortune triumphing over four kings. The set piece
introduces the conventional theme of Fortune's fickleness but it
also offers a variety of theatrical pleasures in the visual display
of '*fowre* Kings *with broken Crownes and Scepters, chained in siluer
Giues*', and in the songs and music which punctuate the action.

The visual pleasures and variety of these set pieces use
emblem and allegory to insist on the moral implications of the
action. They build on the visual images to elaborate commonplaces about Fortune's part in human destiny with poetic
imagery drawn from the emblem and complaint traditions:

Behold you not this Globe, this golden bowle,
This toy cal'd worlde at our Imperiall feete?
This world is *Fortunes* ball wherewith she sports.
Sometimes I strike it vp into the ayre,
And then create I Emperours and kings:
Sometimes I spurne it: at which spurne crawles out
That wild beast multitude: curse on you fooles,
Tis I that tumble Princes from their thrones,
And gild false browes with glittering diadems,
Tis I that tread on neckes of Conquerours,
And when like Semi-gods they haue beene drawne,
In Iuorie Charriots to the capitoll,
Circled about with wonder of all eyes,
The shouts of euery tongue, loue of all hearts,
Being swolne with their owne greatnesse, I haue prickt

The bladder of their pride and made them die,
As water bubbles (without memorie.)

                                    (I, i, 99–115)

Fortunatus is offered the choice of all of Fortune's gifts to
humankind and mistakenly chooses riches which are provided
in the form of a magic purse. The magic purse then generates
action which provides the opportunity to discuss and dramatise
the use and misuse of riches.

There is a constant interaction between moral concepts and
their visual manifestations as the action is held together by
recurring visual motifs. Act I, iii opens with a long and elaborate
dumb show of Vice and Vertue accompanied by devils and
nymphes:

> Vice *with a gilded face, and hornes on her head: her garments long,*
> *painted before with siluer halfe moones, increasing by little and little,*
> *till they come to the full* . . . after her comes Vertue *a coxcombe*
> *on her head, all in white before.*

The same figures of Vice and Virtue appear to speak the moral
at Fortunatus's death. In Act I, Vice and Virtue plant emblematic
trees in the ground, and the priest indicates in a song that Vice's
plants flourish while those of Virtue decline. The allegorical
show indicates the eventual outcome of the play but, more
importantly, it offers a startling visual spectacle, drawn from the
traditions of Elizabethan courtly pageants. The localised pleasure
of the spectacle is connected to the main action in Vice's promise
that his apples will

> win some amorous foole to wanton here
> And taste the fruite of this alluring tree,
> Thus shall his sawcie browes adorned bee,
> To make us laugh.
>
>   (I, iii, 90–4)

In Act III, one of Fortunatus's sons abducts the Princess
Agrypyna to a wilderness where he finds the trees of Virtue and
Vice. In another set scene, he eats the fruit of Vice, is transformed

with an ugly horned head and is taught to love Virtue who makes him fair again.

The apples of Vice and Virtue recur in later scene, being sold by Andelocia and his servant Shaddow 'like Irish coster-mongers'. They generate the plot where the Princess Agrypina discovers which of her lovers is true by becoming ugly after she has eaten the apples of Vice. However the theatrical impact of a series of transformation scenes seems more important than the coherence of the moral scheme. In Act IV, Andelocia deforms all the courtiers with the apples of Vice. The moral reflections on courtly life and the folly associated with love evidently lie behind this sequence but it also generates the scene, similar to a common *commedia dell'arte* scenario, in which Andelocia can appear disguised 'like a French doctor' to cure them by various horrible and comic means. This comic tone is startlingly changed in the finale when, in revenge, the courtiers first tease the brothers, leaving them in the stocks but then murder them, leaving a curiously unsatisfactory ending to the play.

Old Fortunatus was adapted for a court performance. After Dekker had been paid two pounds 'for the eande of fortewnatus for the corte',[20] the play was performed before Queen Elizabeth on 27 December 1599. Dekker's alterations were the prologue in which the old men journey to see Eliza, and the final meta-theatrical gesture in which Fortune is placed in the queen's hands. In its visual display, the trees, the music and the special effects, the play owes as much to the tradition of courtly entertainments as to the folk material. Hoy suggests that given the amount Dekker was paid (the equivalent to half the payment for a complete play) the whole of the allegorical frame may have been added for the court performance, leaving the business of Fortunatus and his sons, the magic hat and the ever-full purse, which constituted the centre of the original play for public performance. However the style and design of the play also show that these devices are now available to theatre audiences outside the court. The resources of the Admiral's Men could be used to return court devices to the court itself.

The performance at court created a rather different problem for the playing company. Court shows offered the possibility of a more direct engagement with the audience, seen in Fortune's final submission to the queen. Because it depended on the character of the audience, this relationship could never be entirely under the dramatist's or the performers' control. Generalisations about the corruption of courtly life and the use and misuse of riches which would have been merely commonplace at a public performance, seem to have had a dangerously particular resonance. As Fredson Bowers, the play's modern editor, has shown, Fortunatus's dying speech (II, ii, 200–13) describing the ambitions seen at court and the heavenly protection against traitors afforded to the 'glorious throne' was excised from the 1600 edition as having too close a connection with the ill-fated rebellion of the Earl of Essex.[21]

The play seems not to have remained in the repertory after 1600. W. L. Halstead[22] suggested that by that date 'the play was outmoded for the London theatre audience'. However, it is important to recognise that one style of theatre did not succeed another in a teleological progression. Dekker's *The Shoemaker's Holiday*, set in an albeit legendary and idealised London, was performed in January 1600 in the same court Christmas season as *Old Fortunatus*, suggesting that citizen values and low life realism could happily coexist in courtly taste with visually elaborate spectacle and abstract moralising. They were all part of the dramatic resources to be drawn on as they suited the inclinations of the professional dramatist.

The variety of style and performance of *Old Fortunatus* illustrates the difficulties involved in characterising a particular play as 'popular'. The ballad and folk material sources might support an association with 'the people'. With a shift of emphasis, the play's wide-ranging use of visual and physical effects might make the same connection. However, as we have seen, those effects were also characteristic of courtly shows, and the play itself was performed at court, not perhaps the most obvious location of the 'popular' audience. It is impossible to fix firmly the notion of 'popular' in sources, dramatic form or audience, since we see instead the eclecticism of a professional dramatist, taking raw materials where he found them and selling the product in different markets with possibly different effects.

A similar eclecticism is evident in Heywood's work for the professional theatre. After 1601 he became the principal dramatist and shareholder of Worcester's Men and his work offers a paradigm of 'popular' dramaturgy both in its location in the down-market amphitheatres of the Fortune and the Red Bull, and in its entertainment values. In the contest between popular and élite drama which took place after the establishment of the new boy player companies in their expensive hall theatres, Heywood situated himself firmly with the traditional theatrical styles. In *An Apology for Actors* he deplored

> The liberty which some arrogate to themselves, committing their bitternesse, and liberall invectives against all estates, to the mouthes of Children, suposing their juniority to be a priviledge for any rayling, be it never so violent.[23]

His alternative to the élite style of satiric iconoclasm was a theatre of exciting physical action, a theatre which was a spectacle and an entertainment, a magical vision of unexperienced riches before it was a theatre of ideas.

> to see, as I have seene, *Hercules* in his owne shape hunting the Boare, knocking downe the Bull, taming the Hart, fighting with Hydra, murdering *Gerion slaughtering Diomed*, wounding the *Stimphalides*, killing the Centaurs, pashing the Lion, squeezing the Dragon, dragging *Cerberus* in chaynes, and lastly, on his high Pyramides writing *Nil ultra*, Oh these were sights to make an Alexander.[24]

This delighted celebration of the labours of Hercules as theatrical action is re-created in the extraordinary sequence of plays, drawn from classical legend, the Golden, Silver, Brazen and Iron Age, which were 'Sundry times played at the Red Bull'. In the elaboration of their staging and the sweep of their dramatic scope, these plays show the enormous variety and theatrical potential of the popular theatre, but they also reveal the intellectual and ideological questions which this theatre addressed. The five plays dramatised Heywood's own *Troia Brittanica* which covered the legends of the gods and heroes from the demise of Uranus to the fall of Troy. The problem of covering such vast epochs is solved by dumb show and narration while the stage action gives scope to the passion and violence of the figures involved.

Heywood's ambitions as a writer and dramatist are expressed by the choric figure of Homer who claims

> I am he
> That by my pen gave heauen to Iupiter,
> Made Neptune's Trident calme the curled waues
> Gaue Aeolus Lordship ore the warring winds
> Created black hair'd Pluto King of Ghosts
> And Regent ore the Kingdomes fixt below. . . .
> I was the Muses patron, learning's spring
> And you shall once more heare blind Homer sing.
>
> (III, pp. 5–6)

Homer, the commentator, is in the action to solve the problems of narrative scale since the balance between narration and enactment is not always finely calculated. Some of the most significant events are dispatched in dumb show and the transitions of the story often seem abrupt. However, the style of the enacted scenes shows Heywood moving surely among the whole range of dramatic styles available to him. As well as the physical action of fights, songs and dances, adapted from the elaborate shows of earlier court entertainments, the plays draw eclectically on the styles of the contemporary drama. For example, the story of Saturn's and Titan's contest over Olympian rule which opens *The Golden Age* is first addressed by two lords discussing the succession in the manner of a history play, and then in a formal flyting between the two protagonists. The plot is moved forward with Saturn's plan to kill his children, which is given dramatic reality both in the comic set piece of the clown and the midwife, and then in the domesticated pathos of the scene in which Sibilla, in childbed, mourns the anticipated death of her new-born son. Heywood thus marries the larger project of recounting the virtues of the ancient gods expressed in dumb show with a comic and popular sense of their impact on more recognisably ordinary people.

Early in *The Golden Age*, the notion of Saturn as the founder of civilisation is first represented in his appearance 'with wedges of gold and silver, models of ships and buildings, bows and arrows', but the heroic image is followed by a clown whose monologue admiring the new invention of cooking ends up as a grotesquely funny account of a courtly lady whose indigestion after eating bear pie was cured by eating a mastiff 'which when she had well eaten, the flesh of the mastiffe worried the beare in her belly, and ever since her guts have left wambling' (III, p. 11). The physical horror of the Thyestean banquet – 'brought in, with the limbes of a Man in the service' – creates a kind of grotesque comedy but the action does not dwell on the paradoxes of this mood. Instead, the banquet is juxtaposed with a stage-fight – 'A confused fray, an alarme' – between the followers of Lycaon and Jupiter and then the pace is varied with the love action between Jupiter and Calisto.

The love interest between Jupiter and Calisto, which Heywood later opportunistically adapted into a further play, *The Escapes of Jupiter*, shows Heywood adapting the masque staging of Elizabethan court theatre to the knowing, sexualised witty style of the rival boy players. Calisto has fled from Jupiter's sexual advances to join the chaste sisterhood of Diana and her nymphes. Diana and her nymphes are introduced with a display which could have come straight from a celebration of the virgin queen: 'Enter with musicke . . . sixe Satires, after them all their Nimphs, garlands on their heads, and iavelings in their hands, their Bowes and Quivers: the Satyrs sing' (III, p. 27). This elegant pastoral is, however, subverted by the arrival of 'Iupiter like a Nimph or a Virago' joking about the difficulty of playing a woman's part. Like the boy player Amazons in *Antonio and Mellida* or Day's *Isle of Gulls*, Jupiter's disguise is used as the occasion for misogynist mockery of stereotyped women's behaviour:

> There I strid too wide. That step was too large for one that professeth the straight order: what a pittifull coyle shall I haue to counterfeit this woman, to lispe, (forsooth) to simper and set my face like a sweet Gentlewoman's made out of ginger-bread?

The joke turns on the male god's inability to play the part and mockery at the folly he will stoop to in pursuit of sexual conquest. Where the boy players' dramatists used such episodes as part of a consistently satiric style,[25] in Heywood they are material for variety and diversion. The action moves swiftly on

to the scene of Calisto's rape; elaborately played through at
the end of one act and decorously narrated by Homer at the
beginning of the next (pp. 33–5). Motivation and psychological
exploration and the possibility of satiric application are deflected
by the pace as the action moves rapidly to the next generation
and the story of Archas, Jove and Calisto's son.

The range of different theatrical styles seen in the Jove and
Calisto episodes is typical of the play as a whole. It works on
three different levels: first, the metanarrative of the conflict
between Saturn and Titan, and the succession to Olympus; then
the comic version of that narrative, bringing its concerns down
to earth, equating them with the perennial sexual anxiety caused
by the problem of men knowing their own sons; and interwoven
with this action, the plots of Jupiter's philandering – itself the
source of possible future problems with succession.

The conflict between Saturn and Titan provides not only the
framing action but also the greatest opportunity for display.
Dynastic complexities and mythological material fill the
speeches but they are principally statements of self-identi-
fication, reiterating and so clarifying the nature of the conflict.
The action can be followed through the stage directions alone.
They show Heywood returning to the 'Armes, drum, colours,
and attendants' (see SD p. 36) style of dramaturgy, developed by
Marlowe in *Tamburlaine* and used by Heywood himself in *The
Four Prentices of London*[26] with the additional excitement of
Titan's giant sons and the variety of fighting on offer:

> Alarme. The battels ioine, Tytan is slaine, and his party
> repulst. . . .
> Enter Enceladus leading his Army, Iupiter leading his. They
> make a stand. . . .
> Alarm. They combat with iavelings first, after with swords
> and targets. Jupiter kils Enceladus and enters with victory.
> Jupiter, Saturne, Sibilla, Iuno, Melliseus, Archas, with the
> Lords of Creet. (II, pp. 51–2)

The sheer numbers of actors on stage, the range of their skills
and the variety of costumes create a sense of opulence which was
central to the appeal of commercial theatre and which was even
further elaborated in the sights and shows of the later Age plays.

The piling on of spectacle was not the only skill employed. *The Golden Age* is undoubtedly episodic but the episodes are carefully balanced so as to create both variety of pace and economy of resources. Iupiter's affair with Calisto is echoed in Act IV by his affair with Danae. The nymphs who attended Diana in Act II are transformed, undoubtedly by doubling, into the 'foure old Beldams, with other women' who describe Danae's situation and are comically teased and flattered into giving Iupiter access to her. The familiar story of Jove's appearance to Danae in a shower of gold is translated into available theatrical possibilities. '*Hee puts off his disguise*' (III, p. 67 SD) in order to appear 'in the high Imperiall robes of Creet' and the seduction scene creates the rest of the excitement. Danae's bed is centre stage with 'foure tapers at the foure corners' (p. 67 SD) and the seduction continues to the moment where 'Jupiter puts out the lights and makes unready' (p. 69 SD) at which point 'The bed is drawne in' and the tone immediately shifted by the clown's filler monologue.

The simple and effective organisation of the action and narrative of *The Golden Age* does not preclude larger intellectual questions. The issue of succession, treated across a range of theatrical styles, had political overtones; the clown's treatment of it connects it to the preoccupations with bastardy and the control of the poor which continued to exercise public concern; the sexualised version of the action in Jupiter's love affairs can be read in terms of collective misogynist fantasy in which all the women, from Danae in *The Golden Age* to Helen in *The Iron Age* give in to rape or are its comic victim. The woodcut illustration to *The Iron Age* showing Hector throwing a rock and Ajax heaving a tree, represents their famous and spectacular confrontation at the height of the Trojan War but the fame of that episode in which male bonding through honour transcends the destructive divisiveness of women again evokes one of the popular fantasies at the heart of commercial drama. A similar complex combination of fantasy and display is evident in the sequences with Penthisilea and her trayne of Viragoes in Part II of *The Iron Age*. The group are in some sense similar to the 'foure beldames' of the scenes with Danae, or the show of Diana and her nymphes. They offer a variation on the display of women which has been a constant of this theatrical style. However, the existence of 'Viragoes' also generates the predicable pleasure of a flyting dialogue about the appropriateness of women warriors followed by a duel between Pyrrhus and Penthisilea (pp. 359–60).

The resulting combination of a fully exploited theatrical style and a full account of the main outlines of classical legend create a sort of anthropological version in which classical legend was presented as originating myth, summarised in the spectacular finale of *The Golden Age*:

> Sound a dumbe shew. Enter the three fatall sisters, with a rocke, a threed, and a paire of sheres; bringing in a Gloabe, in which they put three lots. Iupiter drawes heaven: at which Iris descends and presents him with his Eagle, Crowne and Scepter, and his thunderbolt. Iupiter first ascends upon the Eagle, and after him Ganimed. . . .
>
> Sound. Neptune drawes the Sea, is mounted upon a sea horse, a Roabe and Trident, with a crowne are given him by the Fates. . . .
>
> Sound, Thunder and Tempest. Enter at 4 seurall corners the 4 winds: Neptune riseth disturb'd: the fates bring the 4 winds in a chaine, & present them to Aeolus, as their King. . . .
>
> Sound. Pluto drawes hell: the Fates put upon him a burning Roabe, and present him with a Mace, and burning crowne.
>
> (III, pp. 78–9 SD)

The remaining Age plays followed the same pattern of a metanarrative and an action which treated conflict physically and focused dramatic attention on the sexual encounters of gods and heroes. Heywood's eclectic adaptation of earlier dramatic form is seen in, for example, *The Silver Age's* secularised and spec- tacular version of the harrowing of hell used for the rescue of Proserpine:

> Hercules sinkes himselfe: Flashes of fire; the Diuels appeare at euery corner of the stage with seuerall fireworkes. The Iudges of hell, and the three sisters run ouer the stage, Hercules after them: fireworkes all ouer the house. . . .
>
> Hercules fels Pluto, beats off the Diuels with all their fire- workes, rescues Proserpine.   (pp. 159–60)

The comic twin story adapted from Plautus's *Amphitruo* and

perhaps echoing Shakespeare's *The Comedy of Errors* is used in one of the early episodes with Jove and Ganimede, and earlier Hercules plays are echoed in the famous episodes of Hercules's heroic life. In *The Brazen Age*, the episode with Venus and Adonis, like Medea's incantation to the spirits to defend Jason, echoes Shakespeare and, beyond him, Golding's translation of Ovid's *Metamorphoses*. Like the anthologies and dictionaries which lay behind much popular awareness of the classics, the plays provide a compendium of popularised classical knowledge in its modern as well as its ancient versions.

Heywood's re-creation of classical story eschewed the hard terms and complex allegory which was part of the developing intellectual tradition of élite uses of classical material. In *The Brazen Age*, he does suggest the possibility of an allegorical reading of the episode of the Golden Fleece, but it is offered partly as an apologia for the spectacular style of the enactment itself:

> Let none to whom true Art is not deny'd,
> Our monstrous Buls, and magic Snakes deride.
>
> (III, p. 221)

Throughout the Age plays, Heywood offers various explanations which suggest a serious concern about the intellectual claims which this form of theatre could make. In *The Silver Age*, Homer's prologue says he will lay open for the audience

> the Casket long time shut
> Of which none but the learned keepe the key,
> Where the rich Iewell *(Poesie)* was put.

However, by the end of *The Brazen Age*, the figure of Homer is more apologetic and less confident. He acknowledges once again that 'the learned can only censure right' (III, p. 256) and advises

> The rest we crave, whom we unlettered call,
> Rather to attend then iudge; for more than sight
> We seek to please. The understanding eare
> Which we have hitherto most gracious found.

The Iron Age was dedicated to Thomas Hammon of Grays Inn
and in this dedication, Heywood draws precedent for his work
from the early translator of Aristophanes. He acknowledges that
his play 'exceedes the strict limits of the ancient Comedy [then
in use] in forme' (III, p. 260) but is confident that 'it transcends
them many degrees; both in the fulnesse of the Sceane, and
grauity of the Subiect' (III, p. 261).

The final Age play, *The Iron Age, Part II*, was not published
until 1632 and in the address to the reader of the published
version, Heywood doubts 'I know not how they may be received
in this Age, when nothing but Satirica Dicteria and Comica
Scommata are now in request' (IV, p. 351). The Age plays (though
their chronology is a matter for controversy) themselves seem to
move from the confidence of *The Golden Age* to the sense of
decline from heroism evident in the final play. That view of
classical legend was, of course, conventional enough but the
elegaic motif in the final plays seems also a lament for the decline
of the heroic style in the theatre.

Heywood's long-lived success as a theatre professional
depended on his ability to recognise new trends. He adapted *The
Fair Maid of the West, Part II* to fit the new fashion for sexualised
romance, and in *Love's Mistress* he developed the Caroline court
masque style for the commercial theatre as he had earlier adapted the Elizabethan. Nevertheless, in the prologue to *The English
Traveller* he regrets the 'low pitch' of the contemporary drama
with a nostalgia for the 'great Patriots, Dukes and Kings/
Presented for some hie facinorious things'.[27] Similarly the finale
of *The Iron Age, Part II* can be seen as an elegy for the popular
theatre style. In a speech to her looking-glass, Helen echoes
Marlowe's line about the face 'that launched a thousand ships';
however, that style of drama, like that view of the heroine, is
now old 'and Death is ages due' (III, p. 430). Helen strangles
herself and the epilogue is spoken by Ulysses, in terms no longer
confident of the effectiveness of the old theatrical style:

> If hee have beene too bloody 'tis the Story.
> Truth claimes excuse, and seekes no further glory,
> Or if you thinke he hath done your patience wrong
> (In tedious Sceanes) by keeping you so long,
> Much matter in few words, hee bad me say

Are hard to expresse, that lengthened out his Play.
                                              (III, pp. 430–1)

The scope both of Heywood's ambition and his achievement
in the Age plays indicates something of the vitality of early
modern commercial theatre, but also something of the difficulty
of analysing that phenomenon. The Age plays offer classical
material to an audience which was assumed to include the
learned as well as the 'unlettered'. They offer images of an
originating myth, a decline from a golden age of gods and heroes
to the womanising corruption of the Trojan War and its after-
math; they embody public values of honour and physical
prowess represented as much in the physical as the verbal aspect
of the dramas. Moreover in spanning the period after 1608 which
Andrew Gurr suggests 'fixed the different species of repertory
quite distinctly',[28] they both embody and engage in the controversy about the direction that the theatre would take.

The magic illusionism of the commercial theatre style was the
object of scorn and condescension from rival playwrights, both
of the small-scale indoor theatres and of the next generation.[29]
The terms of that scorn and condescension have been uncritically
echoed by many critics since. However, their tendency to equate
episodic dramaturgy and spectacular effects with simple-
mindedness is not borne out in the cultural politics and poetics
of Heywood's plays. They also offered both the latest and the
oldest in theatre technology, their own version of the fashionable
dramaturgy of the private houses, together with a varied and
informative account of famous stories. For however much the
critics, contemporary and modern may wish to separate off the
down-market commercial theatre, it did not exist in a cultural
siding. It interacted with and helped to define the theatre which
came to dominate élite urban culture and both reflected and
contributed to the creation of its popular alter ego.

The popular politics of these plays are rather harder to
determine and it is perhaps for this reason that they have not
received attention from those who read popular drama politically. Their metanarratives of succession and sexual politics,
however, could be connected to some of the generalised political
preoccupations of the period. Brian Gibbons has asserted that
'adult companies at the Red Bull, the Swan, the Rose and the

Hope largely continue to invoke an air of cheerful patriotism and national self-satisfaction'.[30] However, the anxiety at the centre of the Age plays hardly bears that out. Their very celebration of action, their sense that political conflict might be resolved in violent dumb show, has, as we shall see, a special political resonance in the context of Jacobean foreign policy and its complex interconnection of politics and religion.

2
Politics and Performance

I

The cultural politics of professional theatre, its developing relationship with its audience and its interaction with élite culture
raises the question of the extent to which the popular theatre was
also implicated in a politics of opposition.[1] Dekker's use of
millennial Protestant imagery, and his support for the poor and
neglected in both his pamphlets and the passages in the plays
which derive from them, have suggested to many critics[2] that his
work echoes the factional and class politics of a radical Protestant
opposition. Heywood, too, has been connected to the tradition of
drama which 'appealed, if fleetingly and cautiously, to griev-
ances about economic distress among craftsmen, the burdens of
taxation, the exactions and extortions of courtiers, and the city
rich'.[3]

Heywood's explicit statements on the role of culture in
oppositional politics were predictably cautious. In his *Apology for
Actors*, he explicitly rejected the role of political subversive,
insisting on the dramatist's duty to maintain rather than subvert
order in the state:

to teach . . . subiects true obedience to their king, to show

25

people the untimely ends of such as have moved tumults, commotions and insurrections, to present them with the flourishing estate of such as live in obedience, exhorting them to obedience, dehorting them from all traiterous and felonious strategems.[4]

Heywood's statement was made in 1612 but earlier in his career he had been involved, with Dekker and others, in a play which seemed to the censor to violate these principles and which illustrates the complex relations between dramatic production and the politics of the state.

The Book of Sir Thomas More presented the rise and fall of its eponymous hero from his suppression of the Ill May Day riots of 1517, through a representation of his exemplary household to his tragic fall and execution. It offers one of the clearest examples of official censorship in Edmund Tilney's injunction to the authors of the play to

Leaue out ye insurrection wholy and ye Cause ther off & begin wt Sr Tho: Moore at ye mayors sessions wt a reportt afterwards off his good seruice don being Shriue off Londo uppo a mutiny Agaynst ye Lubards only by A shortt report & nott otherwise att your own perilles.[5]

Tilney seems to have been reacting not merely to the presentation of rebellion but to the particular resonances of riots against aliens in the tense political climate of 1592–3, 'the generally agreed date of the composition of the original play', when

after the rejection of a Bill introduced upon request of the London shopkeepers and freemen against aliens selling by retail any foreign commodities, threatening libels were circulated against Flemish, French, Belgian and other foreign residents, ordering them to leave the country.[6]

The scenes of the riot and its ultimate suppression by Sir Thomas More did 'show people the untimely ends of such as have moved tumults, commotions and insurrections' but the dramatisation of the scenes of riot set up a more complex relationship with the audience than this simple political aim allowed. In the additions and alterations to the text we can see the ways in which its five authors negotiated between the play's politics and its theatrical effects, dealing not only with political events but with the ways in which different social groups responded to them. Anti-alien feeling involved more than xenophobia or purely economic self-interest. The Londoners who protested against the presence of strangers feared for their livelihoods but they also seem to have resented the way in which the king's protection allowed the strangers to treat their hosts in a high-handed manner, defying the city's right to regulate its own affairs.

The opening scene, for example, draws on Holinshed's account[7] of the curious affair of a goldsmith's wife who was abducted by a stranger who then insulted her husband. The scene opens with 'a lustie woman' vehemently resisting the foreigner 'haling her by the arme':

> away ye Rascall, I am an honest plaine Carpenters wife and thoughe I have no beautie to like a husband yet what soeuer is mine scornes to stoupe to a stranger: hand off then when I bid thee. . . .
> Compell me ye dogges face? thou thinkst thou hast the Goldsmithes wife in hand, whom thou enticedst from her husband with all his plate, and when thou turndst her home to him againe, madst him (like an Asse) pay for his wife's boorde. (6–13)

Doll's passionate vulgarity creates instant dramatic interest which draws on her clear differentiation of her self from the goldsmith's wife whose plight might have required more complex dramatic treatment. Her resistance invites sympathetic identification, while at the same time indicating the absolute inalienable rights of an individual which extends beyond status or beauty. In the following sequence, Doll's husband enters quarrelling with another foreigner over a pair of doves bought at the market. As in Holinshed, the foreigner insists that his superior status gives him the right to food of this kind: 'Beefe and brewes may serue such hindes, are Piggions meate for a coorse Carpenter?' (22–3). Doll, in response, insists again on the ·

absolutes on which individual integrity depends: 'what, one stranger take thy food from thee, and another thy wife? bir Lady flesh and blood I thinke can hardly brooke that' (28–9). The men's allegiances make them feel 'curbed by dutie and obedience' but Doll finds in the subordinate status of women, the legal loophole which makes her action possible.[8]

> Ile call so many women to myne assistance, as weele not leaue one inche untorne of thee. If our husbands must be brideled by lawe, and forced to beare your wrongs, their wiues will be a little laweless, and soundly beate ye. (51–3)

Doll's insubordination echoes the comic tradition of unruly women; an effect which is reinforced when she appears in the main riot dressed 'in a shirt of Maile, a head piece, sword and Buckler, a crewe attending' (411, SD). However, she is also contemptuous of the men's cowardice and offers a comic version of Sir John Lincoln's eloquent exhortation to those

> whose free souls do scorn
> To bear th'enforced wrongs of aliens
> (II, i, 4–5)

This presentation of the rebels makes it impossible to close off all sympathy for them. However, the violence of their resistance is equally evident. An incomplete scene in the original version presents a group of 'three or foure Prentises of trades, with a paire of Cudgelles' (452, SD). Their dialogue is all comic bravado and local topical reference, theatrical pleasures with little resonance outside the immediate scenes in which they appear. On the other hand, the scene in which the rebels narrowly escape the gallows offers both an image of the king's mercy and the élite condescension towards the misguided lower orders together with a measure of dignity for the victims. It is very carefully constructed so that Lincoln, the ringleader, is hanged before the pardon comes. But the traditions of representation of scaffold scenes which the playwrights automatically follow, provide Lincoln with considerable dramatic status. The original text of the rebels' punishment presents the full force of retributive justice with a gallows displayed on stage. One of the officers even tries to circumvent the public nature of the occasion by suggesting that they

> Giue it out abroade
> The execution is deferd till morning
> And when the streets shall be a little cleerd,
> To chaine them up and suddenly dispatch it.
>
> (603–6)

In this context both the politics and the dramatisation shifts towards opposition and Lincoln is given a 'gallows oration' which works simple ironies to considerable effect:

> This the olde prouerbe now compleate dooth make,
> that Lincolne should be hangd for Londons sake.
> A God's name, lets to woorke: ffellowe, dispatche,
> (*he goes up*)
> I was the formost man in this rebellion
> And I the formost that must die for it.
>
> (611–15)

Lincoln's brave acceptance of his wrong-doing is endorsed by Doll who twice reasserts the values of personal integrity which formed the basis for her resistance from the beginning. Her own heroism in asking to die before her husband and the simple gesture of their parting on the gallows ladder is most affecting. She is bravely resigned to More's apparent treachery in foregoing the amnesty originally offered:

> Well he is worthy of it, by my troth,
> An honest, wise, well spoken gentleman,
> Yet would I praise his honesty much more
> If he had kept his word and saved our lives.
> But let that pass, men are but men, and so
> Words are but words and pays not what men owe.

The dramatic tone and style of the original version were, however, altered by the additions which were made to the manuscript after it was handed to the players.[9] The scenes of rebellion were most affected by the addition of a clown by hand

B (thought to be Heywood) and the famous additions by hand D (thought to be Shakespeare) in which More quells the rebellion and promises an amnesty to the rebels. The clown interrupts the serious business of Lincoln's oration with bursts of nonsensical bombast which nevertheless engages the audience directly in the events on stage. Though he is urged to let Lincoln speak, he responds with the cheer leading technique of the rhetorical question and the encouraged response:

> Doo all they what they can! Shall we be bobd braue? No!
> Shall we be hellde under? No!
> We are free borne and doo take skorne to be used so.
> (Addition II, 7–10, author's punctuation)

The potential audience responses offered by different groups on stage combine cheerful enjoyment of the excitement, frustration at being prevented from hearing Lincoln, with perhaps some of the élite characters' condescension towards the clown's simple-mindedness. The comic tone of the riot scenes may trivialise the serious political theme, but it offers in return, more various kinds of theatrical pleasure.

These other forms of theatrical pleasure are especially evident in the addition of clown speeches to the gallows scene. His interventions are as pathetic as comic:

> SIR AND I HAUE A SUITE TO YOU TOO . . . THAT AS
> YOU HAUE HANGD LINCOLN FIRST & WILL HANGE
> HIR NEXTE SO YOU WILL NOT HANGE ME AT ALL

The pathos is partly built up in order to create a greater and more exiting contrast with the last minute reprieve, but it also contrasts the rebels' integrity, however mistaken, against the brutality and perfidy of the city authorities.

The representation of rebellion, however, is further complicated by the very different style of these additions which, rather than simply adding an alternative voice, alter the tone of Lincoln's own speeches. The poetic eloquence of his speeches in the rebellion scene are reduced to an empty prose rant, stressing purely economic motives, turning violent xenophobia into a matter of parsnips and red herrings. The rioters who at the beginning of the play and in the early riot scenes had been separately characterised, are reduced to a mass, responding under the speech heading 'All' with only Lincoln, the ringleader, and Doll, the comic relief, differentiated for dramatic purposes.

In contrast to this simplemindedness, More is provided with a powerful speech in which he offers both a vision of the desolate and homeless strangers and an eloquent plea for the inter-dependence of all peoples in the name of common humanity. The power of his eloquence is effective both in theatrical and political terms but Doll's reaction indicates a further dimension of More's authority. In spite of her enthusiasm for a fight, she is mollified by More, less because she is convinced by the arguments of his political theory than because he was at the head of a patronage network which included her family:

> Letts heare him a keepes a plentyfull shrevaltry, and a made my Brother Arther watchins Seriant Safes yeoman lets heare shreeve moore. (Addition II, 165–7)

Social relations in early modern London, even in situations of conflict between élite and subordinate groups, were mediated through the networks of patronage and regional associations which provided 'the middle term between feudal homage and capitalist cash nexus'[10] reinforcing vertical systems of social organisation and complicating the oppositions of interest and wealth. This touch of detailed local colour gave a characteristic density to Shakespeare's representation of the rebels which is more confused elsewhere in the play.

The inconsistency in the characterisation of the opposing groups is a mark of the problems of multiple authorship.[11] Shakespeare may have been asked to work on the play because of his successful presentation of rebellion in *Henry VI, Part 2* but the desire to overrule censorship may have adversely affected the dramatic considerations for the play as a whole. Janet Clare has suggested that

> the recast form of the insurrection serves to illuminate the kind of strategies which playwrights employed to circumvent censorship in an attempt to maintain a measure of dramatic integrity . . . the danger of actual violence is tempered by the

clown's absurd exhortations and the humour serves to defuse the effects of the rioters aspirations. . . . Gestures have been made towards diminishing the censor's underlying apprehensions; the rebels have been discredited whilst the rebellion itself, vital to the play's theatrical life, has been preserved.[12]

Controversy over the additions has centred on the point at which they were inserted. Most recently, Gabrieli and Melchiori have suggested that they may have been added before the play was sent to the censor on the grounds that Tilney's objection to the rebellion was unequivocal and the playwrights could not have imagined that tinkering with tone would have sufficed. They suggest, moreover, that the changes were as much theatrical as political. The apprentice scene, written by Dekker, and inserted before the scene with Lincoln was also excised, together with the only real evidence of violence in the stage direction 'Enter John Munday, hurt'. The apprentice scene, together with the scene with John Munday would have required additional speaking-parts and affected the doubling arrangements in a play with an already unusually large cast. Alterations later in the play, moreover, speed up and smooth the links in the scenes in Sir Thomas More's household, suggesting theatrical rather than political concerns.

Scott McMillin has also suggested that theatrical evidence can refine our sense of political drama in the period. He uses the evidence of the unusually large cast together with the particularly long and demanding central role, as evidence that the play was planned for performance by Lord Strange's Men. According to McMillin, the play suited their repertory because of its political emphasis on individual rights within the framework of an ordered society. Contrasting Lord Strange's Men with the Queen's Men, he suggests:

> Some of their plays are conservative in a stern, steel-ribbed, moralistic mode. . . . This is not the political conservatism of the Queen's men. It is a moral and religious conservatism which in the aftermath of the Martin Marprelate uproar of the late 1580s would have seemed provocative and bold.[13]

This sense of moral and religious conservatism is certainly

borne out in the action involving Sir Thomas More. It is also foreshadowed in the human integrity of the rebels as they fight for their rights and bravely, if simplemindedly, face the consequences. Dekker's apprentices have a certain dramatic individuality, and Heywood's clowns, here as elsewhere, represent the fears of the common man which need not be despised even if they are expressed in comic terms. The relationship between the characters on stage and their audience in the theatre, though in no way endorsing rebellion, could nonetheless allow for the assertion of individual rights and a sense of pathos at the threatened loss even of a foolish clown and certainly of such a dynamic figure as Doll or Lincoln. Their individuality is constructed in terms of class and social status, their location in a system of patronage or in opposition to oppression, whether from foreigners or from a aristocratic élite.

In the event, the play was probably never performed and it is impossible to resolve finally the dating of the additions. What the text reveals is a complex response to political drama. Social conflict provided political and theatrical material. Different artistic responses to its representation provided the opportunity for different kinds of dramatic effect – scenes of comedy or pathos or suspense – in which politics posed theatrical problems and theatrical solutions had political implications.

II

The censor's reaction to *The Book of Sir Thomas More* gave a clear signal that the direct representation of rebellion, particularly when it had topical force, was unacceptable. Nevertheless, the professional theatre dramatists continued to deal with rebellion, most notably in *Sir Thomas Wyatt* and *Edward IV*. The rebellions they dramatised may have seemed less immediately threatening because their underlying politics dealt with less immediate and dangerous tensions. In *Edward IV*, the rebellion was embedded in the dramatisation of heroic citizen values, and in *Sir Thomas Wyatt* the action centred on the more acceptable ideology of antipopery.

Antipopery provided dramatists with a vital source of dramatic conflict as well as providing an appropriate accessible imagery with which to colour oppositions between heroes and villains. This is not to suggest that antipopery was not a real political issue

> There really was a popish threat to the autonomy of Protestant England for much of Elizabeth's reign. Under James, the war with Spain ended but . . . if the alarm over the Spanish match is added to the traditional list which stretches from the Armada, through the gunpowder plot, the various invasion scares of the 1620s and the Irish revolt, then every generation of English people between the 1580s and the 1640s had personal experience of a popish assault on English independence . . . popular antipopery was the product of Puritan or educated Protestant attempts to organise and enlist for their own purposes deep-rooted popular traditions and ways of looking at the world.[14]

For Dekker and Heywood, as for many of their contemporaries, the ideology of antipopery was most available in the huge compilation of Protestant hagiography, *Foxe's Book of Martyrs*. Foxe's accounts of the struggle to establish Protestant monarchy and the heroism of ordinary people in defending their religion gave historical narrative a particular emotional resonance. Dekker and Heywood enlisted this tradition for the repertory of the companies financed by Henslowe in the early years of the seventeenth century. In October 1602, for example, Henslowe paid Dekker and Heywood, together with Chettle, Wentworth Smith and John Webster, for 'a playe called Lady Jane'. The play which Henslowe paid for has been identified as *Sir Thomas Wyatt*, published in 1607, which includes the story of Lady Jane as its framing action, though the uncertain state of the text makes it impossible to ascertain how close the extant play is to the various versions suggested in Henslowe's references both to it and to another 'play of the overthrow of the rebels'. In combining the pathetic story of Lady Jane Grey with a plot of rebellion against the crowned monarch, the dramatists may have been making the most of a random assortment of material, but the text as it stands illustrates the complex relationship between history and dramatic materials with which they worked.

The story of Lady Jane Grey dealt with the unsuccessful

attempt to crown her after the death of Edward VI and thus pre-empt the accession of the catholic Mary Tudor. Lady Jane's martyrdom, as it was presented by Foxe,[15] could be dramatised as a tale of pathos and victimisation, addressing its audience in familiar moral and emotional terms. It also raised the more dangerous question of rebellion against a crowned monarch. Wyatt's rebellion in 1554, according to Antony Fletcher 'came nearer than another other Tudor rebel to toppling a monarch'.[16] However, the dramatists attempted to disentangle the two issues by presenting Jane and her betrothed, Lord Guilford Dudley, as the victims of the machinations of their more politic fathers, so that emotional appeal of their story neutralises the politics of rebellion into the more generalised antithesis between worldly ambition, and the transience of earthly glory.

Following the death of Edward VI, Suffolk plans to place his daughter Lady Jane Grey on the throne and his effort to ensure the continuity of the Protestant line is supported by Northumberland. Sir Thomas Wyatt is appealed to for his support, but at this stage takes the role of political mediator, supporting the official succession of 'those Princely Maides' (I, i, 30) and begging the question of the connection between succession and religious politics. In this way, machiavellian courtly manoeuvring is opposed to the simple concept of undisputed and rightful inheritance. Since Northumberland's plots are so easily foiled, this episode may seem a false start in the play (and with its multiple authorship, this is a serious possibility). Nevertheless it generates scenes in which a simple opposition between honour and politics is at the heart of the dramatic action.

This opposition between politics and honour confuses the lines of dramatic sympathy. The politics of Northumberland's opposition to the rightful monarch are neutralised by the pathos of the way his defeat is dramatised. In Act II, ii, in a last attempt to proclaim the right of Jane Grey, Northumberland calls for a Herald:

> *A Trumpet sounds, and no answere.*
> *The Herald sounds a parlee, and none answers.*
> (II, ii, 19, SD)

As the sound of the trumpet dies away, Ambrose enters to tell

Northumberland that 'the lords have all revolted from your faction' and calls for a second Herald to proclaim Queen Mary's triumph. On this occasion, the herald is answered, *'Within a shoute and a flourish'*.

For Northumberland, this rejection of Lady Jane's claim is tantamount to a rupture in his very identity. He tells Ambrose 'My selfe will now reuolt against my selfe', and as the people respond to the proclamation of Mary's accession, he concedes

> Amen, I beare a part,
> I with my tongue, I doe not with my heart.

The dramatists are using a model for dramatising the fall of a great man, regardless of his position in the politics and the narrative of the play. He enquires ingenuously after his false friends, accepts his crime and hopes for mercy

> when all the soules
> Stand at the bar of justice, and hold up
> Their new immortalized hands.

The localised dramatic effect is, as a result, pathetic rather than condemnatory.

The imagery and dramatic effects in the scene where Northumberland's fellow conspirator Suffolk meets his end, complicates the situation even more. His servant Holmes betrays him with a Judas kiss and then kills himself in grief-stricken repentance. The speed of the sequence allows no dramatic elaboration though it deals with the complicated conflict between allegiance to a master and allegiance to the crown. In Heywood's 1631 history, *England's Elizabeth,* the perfidious servant is vilified in the description of how he

> engaged himselfe with millions of oathes for the performance of his truth and fidelity, yet easily corrupted with some small quantity of gold and many large promises, *Iudas*-like betrayed his Master.[17]

The moral absolute of loyalty and the Christian imagery of the Judas kiss turn Suffolk's betrayal into heroic martyrdom which suggests the tantalising possibility of sympathy for rebellion, a sympathy generated in part by the dramatists' drawing on available conventions of imagery and representation for dramatising the fall of great men.

Both the politics and the dramaturgy are further complicated by the intervention of a clown who watches Holmes strangle himself and then mockingly comments to the audience: 'So, so, a very good ending, would all falce Seruants might drinke of the same sauce.' The rebellious noblemen are condemned but the clown's casual violence also presents a powerful image of the inevitable end of disorder:

> Gold, you are first mine, you muste helpe to shift my selfe into some counterfeite suite of apparel, and then to London: If my olde Maister be hanged, why so: if not, why rusticke and lusticke: Yet before I goe, I doe not care if I throwe this Dog in a ditch: come away dissembler. (II, iii, 84–90)

The clown's violent opportunism cannot offer a viable point of sympathy and the sequence as a whole, indicates the difficulty of translating complex political issues into appropriate dramatic form.

A similar negotiation between political and dramatic coherence is evident in the representation of Wyatt's own rebellion. Unlike Northumberland and Suffolk whose rebellion is motivated by a combination of religious and factional interests, Wyatt rebels in the name of nationalism and English honour, and the text allows a full dramatic exploration of the conflicting political motives involved. When Winchester proposes the Spanish match, Wyatt protests:

> Is shee a beggar, a forsaken Maide,
> That she hath neede of grace from forraine princes?

and insists that Winchester's proceeding is 'policie deare Queene, no loue at all' (III, i, 136). His decision to rebel is taken as a direct consequence of the queen's commitment to the Spanish match and the soliloquy in which the decision is taken, works through the contradictory loyalties to sovereign and nation:

> And ere he land in England, I will offer
> My loyall breste for him to tread upon.
> Oh who so forward Wyat as thy selfe,
> To raise this troublesome Queene in this her Throane?
> Philip is a Spaniard, a proud Nation,
> Whome naturally our Countrie men abhorre.
> Assist me gracious heavens, and you shall see
> What hate I bear unto their Slaverie.
> Ile into Kent, there muster up my friendes.
> To save this Countrie, and this Realme defend.
>
> (III, i, 157–66)

The historical Wyatt asserted at his trial 'before the Judge of all Judges, I never meant hurt against her highness person'.[18] By using the rhetoric of nationalism and freedom, Wyatt's soliloquy similarly complicates the politics of rebellion against the monarch. However, its theatrical power is supported by a shift in the politics of the action. Mary appears at her most autocratic in this scene as she prepares to restore the monasteries and dismisses Arundel's reminder of her oath with a clear assertion of the rights of monarchs over their subjects:

> But shall a Subiect force his Prince to sweare
> Contrarie to her conscience and the Law?

The potentially powerful opposition between corrupted monarchy and the reluctant traitor is, however, not fully carried through in the drama. A residue of the queen's earlier characterisation as the royal victim remains in the reminder that the restoration of the monasteries is to be undertaken at the queen's personal expense. The catch-phrase 'Better a poore Queene, then the Subiects poor' (III, i, 17 and 34–5) is repeated twice, blurring the outlines of sympathy which the narrative requires.

The ambivalent dramatic effect of these scenes demonstrates the discursive complexity which an episodic dramaturgy allows. It reproduces certain conventions of representation which carry contradictory political resonances as they negotiate the problems of aristocracy within monarchy and the limits of popular support. Those limits are dramatised even more fully in the scenes of the rebellion itself. By eliminating Wyatt's fellow

conspirators, Sir James Croft and Sir Peter Carew, the
playwrights kept the issues of the rebellion more clearly focused
on the relations between different orders in society. In the scenes
in Kent, the handling of the common people is turned into a test
of Wyatt's leadership. Before the gates of Rochester, he reiterates
the anti-Spanish appeal, calling

> Hee that loues freedom and his Countrie, crie
> A Wyat: he that will not, with my heart
> Let him stand foorth, shake handes, and weele depart.
>
> (IV, i, 23–6)

The soldiers, of course, reply 'A Wyat, A Wyat, a Wyat!'.

Popular support was not unambiguously an advantage to a
rebellious aristocrat and the dramatic form again modulates the
acceptable sympathy for antipopery to the more problematic
low-life anti-alien feeling. In Act IV, ii, Bret, one of Norfolk's
followers converts his regiment to Wyatt's cause. He does so by
invoking anti-Spanish feeling in a bawdy comic set piece using
a tantalising question and answer routine used by the clown in
The Book of Sir Thomas More

BRET. And wherefore is *Wyat* up?

CLOWN. Because he cannot keepe his bed.

BRET. No, *Wyat* is up to keepe the Spaniards down, to keepe
King *Phillip* out, whose comming in will giue the Land such
a Phillip, twill make it reele agen.

CLOWN.A would it were come to that, a would, wee wold
leaue off Philips and fall to Hot-cockles.

BRET. *Philip* is a Spaniard, and what is a Spaniard?

CLOWN. A Spaniard is no Englishman that I knowe.

BRET. Right, a Spaniard is a Camocho, A Callimancho, nay
which is worse, a Dondego, and what is a Dondego?

CLOWN. A Dondego is a kinde of Spanish Stockfish, or poore
Iohn.

BRET. No, a Dondego is a desperate Viliago, a very Castilian,
God blesse us. . . . A Spaniard is cald so, because hee's a
Spaniard: his yard is but a span.

CLOWN. That's the reason our Englishwomen loue them not.

BRET. Right, for he caries not the Englishmans yard about

him, if you deale with him looke for hard measure: if you
giue an inch hee'le take an ell: if he giue an ell, youle take
an inch. (IV, ii, 420–3)

His performance has comic gusto but, as in *The Book of Sir
Thomas More*, the play distinguishes between low-life xenophobia
associated with anti-alien disturbances and the honourable
nationalism of his leader. The dangers, as well as the strengths
of popular support are economically dramatised, but the force of
the dramatisation holds the two in an uneasy equilibrium.

Wyatt's ultimate defeat takes place off-stage after he has been
abandoned by his soldiers, and the citizens of London have
failed to join the rebellion. However, sympathy for the rebel if
not his cause is created by linking the pathetic ends of Wyatt,
Lady Grey and her lover Guilford. His final soliloquy in particular, gains sympathy for Wyatt in its generalised opposition
between the politic schemes of 'periured Counsellors' and
'innovators' and the honour embodied in Wyatt's heroic desire
'to keepe Spaniards from the land'.

In these final sequences, Wyatt comes closest to a tragic figure
(the lessons of *Richard II* and *Henry VI* are evident) since the
tragic devices of soliloquy and contemplative irony are in play.
However, the overall political impact of the play does not oppose
the stoic individual to the corrupt and repressive monarch, for
this is a politics of negotiation among contradictory alternatives,
aware of the realpolitik of competing hierarchies and the establishment of legitimate authority.

III

In the early years of the seventeenth century, these questions
were part of a pressing political reality. In its invocation of
nationalism and loyalty to an ideal of monarchy, Wyatt's
rebellion dangerously echoed that of Essex. As Mervyn James
has shown.[19] Essex's courtly followers were united by their
opposition to the 'oppressive and corrupting influence of an
upstart and therefore unnatural regime' represented by the
Cecilian faction which barred the natural élite of the nobility
from the queen's person. The citizens of London, too, were

attracted to these ideals of honour and the law of arms. They hoped for militant Protestantism from this flower of the nobility and gentry of England and at the moment of the rebellion. Essex, like Wyatt, appealed to their nationalism, shouting 'that the realm was sold to the Spaniard' as he made his way through Ludgate to the City. In the event, the City did not rally to his support: the citizens were more content to see Essex's opposition to the faction surrounding the queen as symbolic and were not prepared to support a military coup with force of arms. The rebellion itself, in spite of Essex's continued claim of allegiance to the queen, was seen as a breach of civil order which could not be tolerated and certainly not supported.

Nevertheless, after his death, Essex's symbolic role as a focus for oppositional values was paradoxically reinstated:

> A reaction in his favour set in, which promoted the survival both of his faction and of the radical attitudes (in a suitably modified form) and policies (like the anti-Spanish Protestant crusade) which had been characteristic of the Essex House circle.[20]

IV

This complex of popular Protestantism and a 'culture of honour' in relation to the expectations of the aristocracy, combined with antipopery to form the bedrock of Dekker's and Heywood's political drama. It is especially evident in the paradigm myth of antipopery, the story of Queen Elizabeth herself. In *If You Know Not Me You Know Nobody*, Heywood dramatises Foxe's version of the story and, by ending with the queen's accession, celebrates the triumph of the Protestant cause. Political allegiances are made clear, but the politics are always turned into dramatic emotion. From the early scenes, Elizabeth is at the centre of the play's sympathy. Political justification is given dramatic life by characterisation which offers the right blend of imperious dignity – 'We are not pleased with your intrusion, lords' and victimised pathos. When Mary's servants come rudely to summon Elizabeth to Westminster, she appears 'in her bed' (I, p. 200 SD) and the attendant doctors insist that her illness makes it dangerous to fulfil Mary's command. Nevertheless, she offers no opposition:

> The Queen is kinde, and we will striue with death
> To tender her our life.
> We are her subiect, and obey her hest.
> Good night: we wish you what we want – good rest
> (I, p. 201)

When Elizabeth is arraigned by Winchester and Suffolk she is presented, in her own words, as a 'Virgin and a martyr'. The rhetoric of innocence, true royal blood and commitment to true religion are all used to sustain her image and make her not only a powerful political icon but also a powerful presence on the stage.

This combination of politics and theatre is especially evident in the low-life characters who comment on the action. The white coats sent to guard the imprisoned queen acknowledge that they have no right to deal in state affairs:

> But beware of talking of the Princess. Lets meddle with our kindred; there we may be bold.
>   Well, sirs, I haue two sisters, and the one loues the other, and would not send her to prison for a million. Is there harm in this? Ile keepe myselfe within compasse, I warrant you; for I doe not talke of the Queene; I talke of my sisters. Ile keepe myselfe within my compas, I warrant you. (I, pp. 209–10)

Heywood's efforts to 'keep within compas' also dramatises politics as human dilemma. Like Foxe, he combines political events and human responses so as to naturalise the politics of Protestantism. The stories of Elizabeth's kindness to the child who brings her flowers and his heroic defiance against her gaolers, the comic incident in which a goat is brought into where she is imprisoned and her gaoler alarmed at the report of her conversation with a greybeard; the legendary entrance into the tower, the comparison between queen and milkmaid are all taken from Foxe's compilation.[21]

The use of Foxe provided the dramatists with source material which turned complex events into simple scenarios of heroes and villains. Foxe recounts that Elizabeth was 'guarded with a sort of cut-throats which ever gaped for the spoil'[22] and describes in detail how the constable of the Tower denied her the use of her own servants to prepare her food. These moments are dramatised in the simplest inset scenes, sometimes without even any dialogue, where 'Enter the Clown beating a Souldier' (p. 218) or the cook, ordered to make no distinction between the princess's meals and the constable's, enters 'beating a soldier'. This is the emblematic dramaturgy of the morality plays: the anonymous clown stands for Elizabeth's popular supporters and acts as a vehicle for popular feeling as well as the source of dramatic variety. When the soldiers come to collect Elizabeth from Framingham, the clown comically rushes on stage in a comic panic at the sound of their drums. In another set-piece scene of gratuitous knockabout, he pulls the chair of state from under Beningfield, Elizabeth's gaoler, who has impudently sat upon it to pull off his boots! This popular feeling also has a nationalist dimension in the scene between 'An Englishman and Spaniard' when an anonymous Englishman refuses to give the Spaniard the wall, beats him and is then treacherously killed. It encapsulates the politics of the play in the simplest symbolic oppositions of fights and comic violence, a secular version of the psychomachia of morality drama.

The scenes with Elizabeth also draw on and reinforce the popular hagiography which surrounded the memory of the great Protestant queen. In the scene where Elizabeth famously refuses to enter at the Traitor's Gate, the symbolism of the event is insisted upon in order to establish Elizabeth's innocent appeal. She faints and is refused a chair so she sits on the cold stone and allegorises the gloomy weather. In her speech, she turns herself into an emblem of pathos for the benefit both of the gentlemen who escort her and the audience in the theatre:

> See, gentlemen,
> The piteous heauens weepe teares into my bosom.
> On this cold stone I sit, raine in my face;
> But better here then in a worser place,
> Where this bad man will leade me.
> Clarentia, reach my booke.
> Now, lead me where you please, from sight of day,

> Or in a dungeon I shall see to pray.
>
> (I, p. 213)

Elizabeth is presented with pathos appropriate to a dramatic character but with full theatrical acknowledgement of her status not only as England's queen but as God's agent in the defence of true religion.

The tension between Elizabeth's personal fate and her symbolic historical role is resolved by using emblematic dumb show, creating moving pictures which dramatise both the danger besetting the princess and the assured support of God.

Near the end of the play, the queen, at a low point in her fortunes, fears her imminent death. In the inserted dumb show:

> Enter Winchester, Constable, Barwick and Fryers: At the other door, two Angels. The Fryers step to her, offering to kill her: the Angels drive them back. Exeunt. The Angel opens the Bible, and puts it in her hand as she sleeps. Exeunt Angels. She wakes. (I, p. 228 SD)

When she opens the bible it reveals the text: 'Whoso putteth his trust in the Lord, shall not be confounded.' The scene dramatises the combination of magic and superstition which was at the heart of popular religion in an economical and theatrically telling fashion.

This sense of an action moving by magic rather than by narrative logic or motivation accounts for the play's cumulative structure. Once Elizabeth is released from the Tower, the action moves swiftly to the conclusion. Philip leaves England with no explanation beyond 'affairs of state'; this action is reiterated in dumb show which then concludes with the further dumb show of Winchester's funeral. Within the scene, Poole and Queen Mary are dead too, all reported and commented on by attendant lords. In a final irony, Elizabeth enters, looking for death and sees instead, on the pathway to the court, the arrival of Henry Carew greeting her as the new Queen. The deaths of Winchester, Poole and Queen Mary dramatise the magic inevitability of Elizabeth's accession and also make it possible to close the play on an optimistic note. With her main enemies dead, Elizabeth can assure her subjects that 'some we intend to raise, none to displace' (I, p. 246).

The strand of popular support which had provided comic energy throughout the play has also be to be returned to its proper place. The clown has his share in the merrymaking, preparing faggots for the bonfires of celebration, but he is also reprimanded by Tame for his insubordinate failure to weep for the deed queen. The rhetoric uses the trope of the transience of earthly glory and the fall of princes, invoked at the fall of both Northumberland and Wyatt. For whatever the political failings of great men, a proper distance must be maintained between them and more opportunist low-life revelling.

This negotiation between a popular politics and a proper sense of hierarchy is conducted earlier in the play in the representation of the most unlikely candidate for sympathy, Philip of Spain. Foxe had described how when Elizabeth was interviewed by Mary, 'King Philip was there behind a cloth and not seen and that he showed himself a very friend in that matter'.[23] Following this hint, the play provides sympathy for him by having Philip acknowledge Elizabeth's greatness, describing how her

> Virtues and endowments of the mind
> Have filld the eares of Spaine.
>
> (I, p. 203)

He urges leniency on Mary's harsh judgement, standing between Elizabeth and her sister's vengeance. This apparent mitigation of nationalist politics comes from the countervailing need to support the notion of aristocratic virtue. Philip swears to punish the Spaniard who has killed an Englishman with treachery and will not heed the constable's politic advice to marry Elizabeth beneath her or to have her assassinated. He is also saved from being the unwitting agent of Elizabeth's death when the plot to have him seal the warrant is revealed by the honest Gresham.[24] He honourably refuses to seal and instead discharges Beningfield of his duties as gaoler, taking the princess with him to Hampton Court.

The play ends with the famous image of Elizabeth welcomed into London by the Lord Mayor who reaffirms the Protestant faith by presenting Elizabeth with a Bible. In the event, the presentation of a bible was more a wishful instruction than an affirmation of a certainty but for the purposes of this play and in the context of James's accession it provides a suitable happy ending while at the same time reminding James of his duties as defender of the Protestant faith.

The first part of *If You Know Not Me* is short for an Elizabethan play, and its final scene chooses a high point resonant with popular political appeal. However, there was additional material on the reign of Elizabeth which appears, somewhat incongruously, in the course of the second part of *If You Know Not Me*, whose main action concerns the celebrated Sir Thomas Gresham and the building of the Royal Exchange. This play is build round the merest scaffolding of narrative and in the general celebration of London and England, and the nostalgic view of the past, 'The Famous Victory of Queen Elizabeth', promised on the title page, has a worthy place. Where Part I ended on the high point of Elizabeth's accession, Part II concludes with a long scene of that other high point of Elizabeth's reign, the victory over the Spanish Armada. The action is presented as a series of monologues in which three posts come with news from the battle scene. Elizabeth's role is restricted to an orchestration of stoic, and then overjoyed, reactions to the events. The elasticity of this form of dramatic writing is evident from the way in which the bones of the scene are extended in the 1632 edition. An opening scene with the mocking Spanish Dons expands on the sequence's irony, if not its suspense, and the first post tells the story of Drake bravely drawing the Spanish fire and saving the English Navy. The overall effect is to present a scarcely dramatised version of the narrative, offering the pleasures of familiar story and heroic poetry.

This method of building a play out of an accumulation of exemplary set pieces once again provides the episodes in which the queen appears. The dramaturgy is economical, using three lords to set a court scene (I, pp. 322–4), praise the queen and provide the necessary background for Dr Parry's plot to kill her, all in the space of fifty lines. The scene of the attempted murder itself is designed to show both the queen's bravery and her mercy and that she is protected by god. As such, it can risk an almost comic structure in which the Parry twice '*offers to shoote,*

but (she) returning he withdrawees his hand'. The queen does eventually realise the danger she is in but remains merciful, leaving
Leicester to overrule her mercy and commit Parry 'to the Tower,
then to death'.

The casualties of this style of dramaturgy are subtlety and
naturalistic characterisation. The queen's enquiry to Parry about
the 'English Fugitivies that seeke my life' is a mechanical
reminder of how Parry first escaped the queen's justice and
weightily underscores the irony of her immediate situation.
Parry's own ingratitude can only be emphasised in a soliloquy
which cannot resolve his action in terms of recognisable naturalist motivation. At the end he can only ask:

> Heauen! what shall I do?
> Euen what Hell and my damn'd heart shall thrust me to.
>
> (I, p. 325)

This sense that the characters are both morally responsible for
their actions and yet providence is the ruling historical force
creates interesting dissonances in the politics of this play. The
queen is given a symbolic radiance, a religious status which
makes it impossible for her to act with any politic involvement
in the affairs of state and yet villains are punished and the
connection between mercy and political skill is discernible but
not emphasised. The dramaturgy thereby re-enacts an important
principle both of Elizabeth's own careful propaganda and a
principal aspect of popular politics: the status of, and loyalty to,
the monarch, especially Queen Elizabeth, is kept secure. The
problem with state affairs lies in the politic machinations of evil
counsellors and ambitious lords. It also permits a populist
distinction between worthy and unworthy followers of a queen,
revealed in the queen's pleasure before the battle of the Armada
that

> I do not see, 'mongst all my troops
> One with a courtier's face, but all look soldier like.
>
> (I, p. 338)

None of the popular audience could aspire to being a courtier
but serving the queen as a soldier was open to all. In drawing

on the mythology of popular politics and presenting it through
the techniques of pathos and comedy drawn from popular
dramaturgy, Heywood, was, in effect, creating an audience for
popular political ideas and constructing the terms in which they
could most effectively be understood.

V

The political resonances of plays about the virgin queen shifted
markedly in the new reign. The accession of James I had put an
end to anxiety about the succession but, in the new reign, the
glorification of Elizabeth as a providential agent of the triumph
of the Protestant cause carried more oppositional force. As David
Riggs has shown, two alternatives were open to those who
dramatised the politics of his accession. They could emphasise
either

> the continuity between the new regime and the old, em-
> phasising James's Protestantism, his English ancestry, and his
> readiness to participate in the national heritage of his new
> subjects [or] the differences between Elizabeth and James,
> emphasising James determination to make peace with Euro-
> pean nations, his plans to unify England and Scotland, his
> imperial status as ruler of the British (and not simply English)
> people.[25]

As the new situation settled it became clear that James preferred
the latter option and both religious and political opposition
settled around commitment to militant Protestant nationalism
centring its hopes on Prince Henry.

These hopes were dashed by the Prince's death in 1613. The
elegies written on his death further defined his symbolic importance. Heywood's *Funerall Elegie* emphasised the importance of
sustaining the young prince's memory and, in the tradition
of the genre, was critical of the world he has left behind. In the
poem's allegory, Pleasure leaves the world and her garment is
taken on by Sorrow which 'deluded/The world with fading
ioyes and transitory'. The allegory holds at bay any suggestion
of precise political dissatisfaction but the analogy with Astrea,

the familiar mythological representative of Elizabeth, is a possible echo. When Pleasure left the world, moreover,

> Honour fled, with it, it beares his tracke
> No Time, nor Age can stay or call him backe.

The shift from Pleasure to Honour makes the political resonance more precise, connecting Prince Henry's honour with the political demands for a more actively anti-Catholic foreign policy: and this notion of honour is made even more pointed in the succeeding stanza of praise for the Prince:

> His Spirits were all active, made of fyre
> Which saue in travell can admit no rest
> High were his thoughts, yet still surmounting hy're
> His very motives Industry profest
> To be in Action was his sole desire
> And not to be so he did most detest.[26]

Dekker's commitment to militant Protestantism is even more marked. His collection of prayers, *The Four Birds of Noah's Ark*,[27] echoes the apocalyptic imagery of militant Protestant writing: the prayer for the King, though utterly loyal, makes his anti-absolutist position clear. Echoing James's contention that 'Kings are gods upon earth', he nevertheless reminds the king that

> they are but thy servants; they rule kingdomes, yet the chariot of their Empire turnes over and over, unlesse thou teach their hands how to holde the bridled. More then men they are amongst men, yet lesse they are then themselves, if they breake thy lawes. (p. 101)

His prayer for active young Prince Henry insists even more explicitly on the importance of a militant Protestantism:

> Religion be the columne upon which hee shall alwayes stand, zeale the pillow upon which he shall kneele, and the quarrel of the Gospel, for which he shall go to warre. (p. 110)

Dekker's firmer commitment to an oppositional politics of

Protestantism was evident in his 'Elizabeth play', *The Whore of Babylon*, published in 1607. In his dramatisation of 'the incomparable Heroic vertues of our late Queene', Dekker took a fierce antipopish stance, directly presenting the conflict between true religion and the whore of Rome as an apocalyptic allegory of a universal struggle. This allegorised conflict between good and evil, tied to very precise political circumstances, is perhaps not to modern taste. However, it offers a triumphant celebration of the politics of popular theatre in the dazzling variety of forms in which they could be dramatised. The action moves in and out of allegory, combining the representations of Truth and Plain Dealing with such historical personages as Campion, the Jesuit scholar, Lopez, Elizabeth's physician and Parry who made an attempt on her life. The Roman church is variously represented by 'Falshood, *(attir'd as Truth is) her face spotted'* (IV, i, SD) and a magnificent dumb show of the 'Empresse on the Beast' accompanied by cardinal and kings (IV, iv, SD). Queen Elizabeth is allegorised in both the figure of Truth who wakens to begin the action, and Titania the Fairy Queen who escapes from and thwarts the stratagems of the Whore.

As well as spelling out the religious and millennial implications of Elizabeth's reign, the allegory also involves social satire. The most dangerous of Elizabeth's opponents are the doctors and scholars of false learning, and the clown figure, Plaine Dealing, presents a convert from the Whore of Babylon's country who brings the life of ordinary people to the attention of the Fairy Queen. He describes how 'I left villains and knaves there, and find knaves and fooles here: for your Ordinary is your Isle of Gulles, your ship of fooles, your hospitall of incurable madmen' (II, i, 87–9). At the end of the play, Plaine Dealing joins forces with Truth 'leading souldiers with drum and colours' to fight the Armada. Plaine Dealing is charged with ridding the camp of corruption and treachery and the ensuing fight contrasts the cowardly Spaniards with Elizabeth's brave 'Captaines, Marriners and Gunners with Linstockes' culminating in the heroic vision of 'Titania in the Camp' where, like Heywood's Elizabeth, she explicitly compares the luxury of a civilian court with the heroism of military kingship.

The attacks on idle courtiers, the contempt for courtly masques seen in Elizabeth's rejection of the first Babylonian

Embassy, and the central role given to Plaine Dealing, provided a myth of identity for the audience of the Fortune where the play was performed. Episodes such as Elizabeth providing succour for the displaced Netherlanders (II, i) or the Babylonian king's efforts to corrupt Elizabeth's servants, gave the satire a more pointed political focus. The play even indulges a fantasy of a worthy successor to Elizabeth who after her death will

> A second Phoenix rise, of larger wing,
> Of stronger talent, of more dreadfull beake,
> Who swooping through the ayre, may with his beating
> So well commaund the winds, that all those trees
> Where sit birds of our hatching (now fled thither)
> Will tremble, and (through feare strucke dead) to earth,
> Throw those that sit and sing there.
>
> (II, i, 235–41)

In the context of James's policy of peace in Europe and his failure to support Protestant struggles in the low countries, the oppositional political message was unmistakable. However, the mythology of Elizabeth was both powerful and commonplace enough to keep the message at the level of fantasy rather than a direct attack on the new regime.

The allegorical action draws on an extraordinary range of sources from biblical and apocalyptic writing, and from the emblematic tradition. It is important to remember that this material was part of a popular tradition as much as the drums and trumpets of the Armada scenes.[28] The emblem of Truth the daughter of Time which is elaborated in dumb show at the beginning of the play had been used as a pageant at Elizabeth's coronation[29] and its full significance involves a complex interlocking set of symbolic codes including classical, historical and millennial ideas to reinforce the sense that Elizabeth's accession was momentous in its fulfilment of prophecy as well as in its immediate political consequences.[30] The physical imagery, moreover often required a negative reading: Falsehood is 'attired like Truth' but her dumb show is explained by Truth herself to indicate the evil intent of her companions symbolised in the props of sword, box and gloves that they carry. For as well as representing evil, the Whore and her companions have to demonstrate its attractiveness and the dangers of falsely falling under its spell. The action is therefore often glossed with a commentary so that the audience, both on-stage and off, realise simultaneously the truth and the seductive power of falsehood.

This dramatic style is occasionally static and the interlocking metaphors and parenthetical phrases of the poetic style, though they reflect the complexity of the ideas, are often difficult to follow. The combination of allegory and action and the density of reference which it embodies indicates the complexity of popular mentalities which informed both popular drama and popular politics. In both his note to *Lectori* and in the play's prologue, Dekker seems to have been defensive about this dramatising of history. In what may have been another thrust at Jonson, he insists 'that I write as a Poet, not as an Historian, and that these two doe not liue under one law'.[31] He seems in the same note to be less than happy with the efforts of the Prince's Men at the Fortune to realise his poetic and political vision

> for let the Poet set note of his Nombers, even to Appolloes owne Lyre, the Player will haue his owne Crochets, and sing false notes, in dispite of all the rules of Musick.

Dekker's concern for the piece is also evident in the way he scolds the audience, asking that

> The Charmes of silence through this Square be throwne,
> That an un-usde Attention (like a Iewell)
> May hang at euery eare, for wee present
> Matter above the vulgar Argument:
> Yet drawne so liuely, that the weakest eye,
> (Through those thin valies we hang betweene your sight,
> And this our piece) may reach the mistery.

In 1607, following the Gunpowder Plot, when *The Whore of Baby-lon* was performed, Dekker could rely on an audience's assent to the dramatic material of antipopery; but his concerns about the ability of popular players to perform and popular audience to appreciate lingers behind the work. For popular theatre to work as a theatre of political opposition requires a more than usually delicate balance of a shared ideology, a familiar and appealing theatrical form to give it life, and conditions of performance which would provide for the widest dissemination. Antipopery provided the ideology, the history play provided the form and the open-air theatres provided the venues in which that balance could be achieved.

3
Prentices, Citizens and the London Audience

I

Dekker and Heywood's history plays focused on the religious conflicts of the preceding century and developed a dramaturgy which could represent popular political concerns. By creating such heroic figures as Sir Thomas Wyatt and an idealised image of Queen Elizabeth herself, they evolved a dramatic language with which to express an emotional commitment to active Protestantism and to dramatise the possibility of popular intervention in national affairs. This dramatic language was often at odds with a systematic political analysis for it endorsed both heroic rebellion and stable monarchy. However, in doing so, it embodied the contradictions of early modern political life. Moreover that contradiction was a result of the plays being driven by theatrical, as much as political considerations. The eclectic use of available theatrical effects, the pathos and the comedy were all mobilised for the action, often in such as way as to work against the plays' obvious political direction. Clown figures, in particular, destabilised the plays' politics by providing a mocking comic perspective on the action which had to be neutralised in their final resolutions.

A similar tension between comic dramaturgy and ideological coherence is evident in Dekker and Heywood's plays which dealt with the glorification of London. They forged a common identity for the popular audience by locating them explicitly as Londoners. *Sir Thomas Wyatt* and the plays about Elizabeth drew on the nationalism of antipopery and addressed the audience as Englishmen. The celebration of the civic life of the capital addressed the audience specifically as *Londoners*, and required a differently inflected treatment of politics and history.

In Heywood's *Edward IV*, a lengthy sequence at the beginning of the play presents Falconbridge's attack on the city of London supported by rebels from Essex and Kent. Its theatrical shape is provided by a number of 'sieges to the tiring house' interspersed, in familiar history-play fashion, by parleys and confrontations between the rebels and the good citizens of London. The resulting dramatic effect created a tension between nationalism and civic pride. Falconbridge claims that he is undertaking rebellion on behalf of 'True hearted English', disenfranchised by 'the sad yoke of Yorkish servitude' and distinguishes his rebellion in the name of 'ancient libertie' from the uprisings of

> Tyler, Cade and Straw
> Bluebeard, and other of that rascal rout
> Basely like tinkers or such muddy slaves
> For mending measures or the price of corne
> Or for some common in the wield of Kent
> That's by some greedy cormorant enclos'd
>
> (I, p. 9)

Falconbridge's distinction between political rebellion and rebellion for economic reasons is clear enough but the rhetoric of his speech creates a certain confusion. The line 'That's by some greedy cormorant enclos'd' is conventional rhetorical padding but it allows the possibility of at least a measure of sympathy for the rural poor who are his followers. This rhetorical confusion suggests the possibility of *political* complexity which is even more evident in the dramatic presentation of the rascal rout itself. It draws on the tradition of comic low-life performance familiar from Shakespeare's presentation of Jack Cade or the anonymous play of Jack Straw.[1] Falconbridge's rabble, Spicing,

Smoke and Chub the chandler of Chepstow, comically echo
his words. Like Bret and his followers in *Sir Thomas Wyatt*,
their readiness to fight and threaten have enormous potential for
ad libbing comic performance and the association with popular
rebellion complicates the political implications of the scenes in
which they appear. It partly undermines the seriousness of
Falconbridge's claim, but it enhances its theatrical impact and
echoes other motifs from contemporary political culture.

Although the Falconbridge coup is led by a politically motivated aristocrat, the play presents the rabble's motives in economic
rather than political terms. They view London as a source of
booty:

> You know Cheapside: there are mercers shops
> Where we will measure velvet by the pikes
> And silkes and satins by the street's whole bredth:
> We'le take the tankards from the conduit-cocks
> To fill with ipocras and drinke carouse,
> Where chaines of gold and plate shall be as plenty
> As wooden dishes in the wilds of Kent. . . .
>
> No sooner in London will we be
> But the bakers for you, the brewers for mee.
> Birchin Lane shall suite us.
> The coster mongers fruite us
> The poulterers send us in fowl,
> And butchers meate without controul:
> And ever when we suppe or dine
> The vintners freely bring us wine.
> If anybody aske who shall pay,
> Cut off his head and send him away.
>
> (I, pp. 10–11)

This doggerel invokes a familiar image of economic disorder[2] but
it is also a carnivalesque fantasy of unlimited consumption.
Spicing has lined the rebels up on the stage and invited them to
share the vision of London's plenty. As such, it has an ambiguous
dramatic impact as both a celebration and an attack on London
and the values of an urban culture on guard against depreda-

tions both from rural invasion and from disorder initiated by the disadvantaged urban poor.

Manning describes how 'Between 1581 and 1602, the city was disturbed by no fewer than thirty-five outbreaks of disorder.'[3] The response of London's ruling orders was partly to guard against economic hardship by importing and distributing food, and partly to enact repressive measures against vagrants and immigrants into the city. Falconbridge's supporters represent both kinds of threat to civic order for although they are supposed to be from Essex and Kent, they are also described as

> those desperate, idle swaggering mates
> That haunt the suburbs in the time of peace,
> And raise up ale-house brawls in the streete.
>
> (I, p. 18)

This description comes in a flighting between Spicing and a pair of apprentices who are keen to take part in heroically defending the city. By setting apprentice against rebel, citizen against suburban, the text minimises the potential for equating populism with rebellion and drives a wedge between different elements within popular culture which is given symbolic physical form in the *'very fierie assault on all sides, wherein the prentices doe great seruice'* (p. 20 SD).

This alignment of apprentices with the ruling élite of the Lord Mayor glosses over the historical conflict between apprentices and the city authorities which lay behind much late Elizabethan civil unrest. Just as Falconbridge rested his claim on history, so the Lord Mayor and the apprentices are connected through their heroic history of allegiance to the crown. When Falconbridge accuses the citizens of treachery towards Henry VI, Shore retorts

> My lord Maior bears his sword in his defence,
> That put the sword into the arms of London,
> Made the lord Maiors for euer after knights,
> Richard depos'd by Henry Bolingbroke,
> From whom the house of Yorke doth claime their right.
>
> (I, p. 15)

The lord Maior too reminds the citizens of the occasion for that honour when Walworth killed the rebel Wat Tyler and the apprentices themselves place their resistance to Falconbridge as part of a history reported by the *Chronicles of England*.

The play deals very gingerly with the dangerous contradictions of popular politics. The city, the apprentices and the crown are marshalled in support of the ideology of rightful monarchy. The allegiance works symbolically in the theatrical psychomachia of the alarums and excursions but the overdetermined insistence of the speeches, the array of ideologically-fraught reference and imagery suggest tensions in the political understanding which are far from completely resolved.

In the rebellion scenes of Heywood's *Edward IV, Part 1* such diverse figures as the Lord Mayor, Master Shore and the heroic prentices who fought the rebels, were united in their opposition to the invading rebellious army. However, as we saw in *The Book of Sir Thomas More*, citizen chauvinism provided no such unproblematic point of identification. The real problems of London, the separation of a ruling oligarchy from an increasingly proletarianised working population, the civic difficulties of regulating both commercial development and the problem of the poor, provided the background tension and political concerns which Dekker and Heywood had to turn into the structures of drama.

As Michael Berlin has shown,

> from the mid-1580s, coinciding with the growth of a 'hot' puritan opposition, increasing concern on the part of the city governors grew into a policy of repression of the more disorderly aspects of popular customs, especially those popular observances associated with rituals of misrule and the inversion of social norms.[4]

However, that awareness of potential civic difficulty was countered by an image of London which denied the city's real social and economic differences in its faith in the coherence of the populace. Stowe, London's great chronicler, for example, asserted that in spite of the increasing number of people excluded from the city's ruling oligarchy, 'whatsoever the number be, it breedeth no feare of sedition: for as much as the same consisteth not in the extremes but in a verrie mediocritie of wealth and riches'.[5] The connection that Stowe made between on the one hand, difference of wealth and, on the other, sedition lay at the heart of civic anxieties. The extent to which it emerged in plays depended on dramaturgic questions of structure and style.

One dramatic realisation was presented in Heywood's *The Four Prentices of London* which placed questions of wealth, religion and nationhood in a fantasy-setting of the crusades. The four prentices of London, in fact noblemen down on their luck, do not scorn to act as apprentices but at the earliest opportunity set off to fight the infidel and win wealth and fair ladies. The scenes are structured by high rhetoric and energetic physical action only tenuously attached to a narrative. In this play, symmetry is more important than characterisation or verisimilitude as each of the brothers is given successive scenes involving spirited encounters in which the brothers and their father constantly cross but only recognise one another in the final scenes. These encounters almost invariably involve fighting: with bandits, with the Soldan and his soldiers, and with one another. The main theatrical appeal is provided by marching and drums, and such colour-effects as the Soldan on the walls flourishing his 'vermilion flag' (l. 1909). At every turn the honour of the prentices is equated with the honour of military valour. In the emblematic style, the theatricality of battle can be glossed by the prentice values as the play brings together in dramatic form, the visual emblems of popular culture with the language which will, as Guy says, 'Historifie my name'.

This question of history and authenticity was crucial to the impact of *The Four Prentices of London*. The prologue to the play is interrupted by three contesting figures who argue about the kind of history they will be enacting. Figure 2 asserts 'If we should not beleeve things recorded in former ages, wee were not worthy that succeeding times should beleeve things done in these our ages' (22–4).[6] His opponent argues 'But what authority have you for your History? I am one of those that wil beleeve nothing that is not in the Chronicle' (25–6). The justification for the history is then given:

> Our authority is a Manuscript, a booke writ in parchment; which not being publique, nor generall in the world, wee rather thought fit to exemplifie to the publique censure, things concealed and obscur'd, such as are not common with every

one than such Historicall Tales as every one can tell by the fire
in Winter. (27–31)

The drama is thus placed in an intermediate position between
popular, oral culture and the official histories of the chronicles.
It gives its audience independent access to scholarly history,
invoking the theatrical pleasures of novelty – 'Had not yee
rather, for novelties sake, see Jerusalem yee never saw, then
London that yee see howerly' (31–3) – alongside the historical
values of truth and tradition.

The textual and theatrical history of *The Four Prentices of
London* is too obscure to reveal whether this concern with history
was a feature of the original or later versions of the play.
Heywood's epistle to the reader of the earliest extant text of 1615
connects the play's publication to the revival of artillery training
for London's prentices which was resumed around 1610 and
reminds us of the difficulty of locating Heywood's work in any
simple relation to the development of dramatic style or changes
in taste. The play seems to have been Heywood's first and may
have been written as early as 1592–4, at the time of the vogue for
prose accounts of heroic prentices. However it became part of the
Worcester's Men repertory and seems to have been revived in
1602, been available for reading in 1607 and been sufficiently
current to be published in 1615. Its vehement support for an
active popular role in religious conflict may well have had an
especial political resonance in the early years of James's reign.

This historical contextualisation complicates the fantasy of
shared aspiration and uncomplicated values in which prentices
and noblemen were the same, wealth was a pot of gold and
marrying a king's daughter raised no political or dynastic
complications. It was a fantasy which Heywood drew on again
in his more ambitious attempt to dramatise the glory of London
in the second part of *If You Know Not Me You Know Nobody* sub-
titled 'With the building of the Royal Exchange AND The famous
Victory of Queen *Elizabeth*: Anno 1588'. The play's title brings
together civic achievement and national glory but the precision
of the dating and the realism of the setting cast the fantasy in a
rather different light.

The episodic plotting and the sense that merchant venturing
is a matter of romantic affairs in foreign parts echo the form of

the simpler 'prentice play'. When Gresham takes up an offer for the Barbary sugar monopoly, the commercial considerations are seen as a matter of personal courage which rebound to his 'credit and your countries honor' (I, p. 253). When the venture fails, he bears the loss with wit and good grace which astonishes those around him. This version of citizen values can be dramatised by emblematic gesture: the romance of merchant venture is summed up in dispatching factors to Barbary, Venice and Portingall; the graceful acceptance of loss in the gesture of dancing in the barbary king's goodwill gift of slippers:

> Come undoe my shoes
> What, 60 thousand pound in sterling money,
> And paid me all in slippers? Then hoboyes, play!
> On slippers Ile dance all my care away.
>
> > (p. 300)

This cavalier disregard for money is regarded as 'royall' by those on-stage who witness it and perhaps by its off-stage audience too. However, the play also acknowledges the possibility of a more complex response. Gresham is made to explain

> I do not this as prodigall of my wealth
> Rather to show how I esteem that losse
> Which canot be regain'd.
>
> > (p. 301)

In the more realistic setting of this London play, the questions of wealth and responsibility and the connection between wealth and exploitation lie behind, and seem to put pressure on the enactment of citizen values. As Laura Stevenson has shown,[7] stories of successful merchants involved working round the contradiction between the complaint tradition in which wealth is the root of all evil, and the glorification of wealth as the source of charity and good works. From the beginning Gresham is described as 'clear from avarice and base extortion' (p. 251). In the story of the building of the Royal Exchange, he is placed in the long tradition of great London men, who defended both the city and the realm, built up its colleges, alms houses and

conduits, and set an example in charity. Gresham's historical
lineage is rather clumsily expounded in a scene where Dean
Nowell shows his friends portraits of earlier London notaries
and offers a brief history of each, including setting the record
straight on Dick Whittington. It offers a fascinating attempt to
deal with the relationship between history and myth in the
popular conception of London of which the play is itself a part.
With this context set, Gresham's own charity can be dramatised
more fully. A storm (presented on stage) prompts Gresham to
plan to build

> such a roofe,
> That merchants and their wives, friend, and their friends,
> Shall walk underneath it, as now in Powles.
>
> (I, p. 268)[8]

Negotiation with the civic authorities is reduced to an
exchange with the symbolic and easily recognisable figures of
the Lord Mayor, Sherrifs and their Sword bearer. The actual
building, too, occurs in symbolic stage action as Gresham, the
Lord Mayor and the shopkeeper Hobson each lay a foundation
stone with a piece of gold for the workmen. Tension between
merchants and the city authorities, between large and small
mercantile interests, and between all of them and those who
laboured for a living, is resolved by symbolism and pageantry:

> Oh God bless M. Gresham! God bless M. Gresham!

Reducing a narrative to set symbolic scenes, however, limits
the scope of its dramatic action and, in order to fill the play, the
action has to be varied by other plots involving Hobson and his
shop, and the trickery of Gresham's nephew John. In these
actions Heywood draws on different, rather livelier dramatic
traditions and the effect is to disrupt the fantasy of the mag-
nanimous merchant seen in the action with Gresham and the
building of the Royal Exchange.

Hobson, the idealised comic shopkeeper, is a kindly, bluster-
ing master with his set phrase 'bones a me' and his disobedient
but good-hearted apprentices. He is introduced in a comic
exchange with country pedlars who come to restock their wares.

The scene is enlivened by bawdy jokes about the Puritan taste in poking sticks, the changeable foreparts of young wenches and the fashion for yellow, the colour of cuckolds. Hobson speaks for the enduring values of honesty and thrift, reminding Gresham of the

> golden world,
> When we were boyes: an honest country-yeoman
> Such as our fathers were, God rest their souls
> Would wear white karsie.
>
> (I, pp. 254–60)

This fantasy of a golden time before markets in luxuries developed contrasts in part with his own trade in fashionable goods but it is also the background to the episode of the legal dispute between Gresham and Sir Thomas Ramsie over a piece of land. Only Hobson the shopkeeper has the sense to see that only lawyers benefit from such quarrelling and with Dean Nowell, persuades the great merchants to come to terms. Dean Nowell's mediation is modelled on an idealised rural life in which village notables could enforce acceptable social norms and Hobson articulates those underlying values in radical political terms:

> all *Adams* earth
> And *Adams* earth is free for *Adams* sons,
> And tis a shame men should contend for it.
>
> (I, p. 267)

Hobson's radicalism is, however, comically ineffective in dealing with the practices of the commercial world. In the scene where Hobson is introduced, he gives goods worth ten pounds to the pedlar, named in his books as 'John Tawny-coat'. When the pedlar returns to pay his dues, he uses his true name 'John Goodfellow' and Hobson refuses to accept the money, which produces a comic argument over who is the most honest. Each accuses the other of madness in offering money and refusing to take it, a comic inversion of more usual commercial conflict.

This brief comic encounter with John Goodfellow is turned in a later scene into a poignant reminder of the real cost of

London's growing wealth. Hobson finds himself in Deptford where he encounters the pedlar who has become destitute because he has been charitable to his neighbours in time of dearth. The earlier connection between John Tawny-coat and Hobson maintains some continuity with the play's narrative but the scene is a symbolic set piece, in which the poor labourer *'with a spade'* speaks for all the poor who are excluded from the new commercial wealth of London. Hobson can act mercifully to him and applauds his thrift but he reminds the audience that in this encounter

> as in a looking glass
> I see the toil and travell of the country,
> And quiet gain of cities blessedness.
>
> (I, p. 305)

A more complex dramatic and ideological alternative to citizen values is presented in the plots involving Gresham's nephew John. He both inherits the characteristics of the medieval Vice and looks forward to the witty young man about town who is both satirised and celebrated in boy player comedy. From the very beginning, John Gresham shows the vice's traditional ingenuity. When Gresham questions him about his 'bad husbandry/Carelesse respect and prodigall expense', he turns his accusations to comic effect, explaining that he seduced his neighbour's wife and gave a gown to a whore, in response to biblical injunctions to love his neighbours and to clothe the poor! When he is sent to collect a hundred pounds from Gresham's puritan factor and his plan to steal it is thwarted, he manages to have the factor arrested by a pair of comic sergeants and tricks him into revealing that his holiness is hypocrisy and he owes his master five hundred pounds.

The scenes with John Gresham are full of a kind of comic excess: the puritan factor spouts proverbs and reminders of the old Marian martyrs; the sergeant and his man Quicke are introduced in a little sequence in which they reveal the tricks of their trade. The direction of the episode is constantly diverted as every character reveals that he is not what he seems. There is a sense of Heywood constantly filling the action with devices rather than driving through character and narrative. Gresham's anger at being tricked turns to amused tolerance at youthful wit:

> afore-god, it hath done my heart more good,
> The knave had wit to do so mad a tricke
> Then if he had profited me twice so much.
>
> (I, p. 282)

The tension between profit and pleasure is resolved in dramatic comedy.

John Gresham's wit provides the comic energy which fills up the rest of the action: he is dispatched to France to act as Hobson's factor and he wastes money and time on whores. Hobson discovers that John is spending his factorship wenching in France, but when he comes to France to investigate, John tricks him into being caught with a whore and he is glad to let him off in return for concealing the prank from his wife. Occasionally the tone of John's plots goes out of control as in the scene when he tries to have Timothy hanged, or in the unpleasantly predatory edge of his encounter with the courtesans. As he cheerfully acknowledges to his uncle, John is a 'new man'. Gresham understands this in the sense that his nephew has reformed his evil ways but John's subsequent behaviour shows that he is 'new' in pushing the logic of mercantile values to their comic and occasionally, their exploitative limit.

The finale of John Gresham's 'trickster' plot shows the dramatic form taking over from the ideological coherence once again. After his defeat of Hobson in France, John appears (p. 327) proposing in soliloquy to restore his shattered fortunes by marrying Lady Ramsie, whose husband, the Lord Mayor, had died a few scenes before. His blatant opportunism is made more comic by his having to hold creditors at bay whose interest in his success is similarly financial. His impudent speech of courtship is comically frank and parodies both the ideals of charity and the familiar joke about remarrying widows:

> madam you are rich, and by my trothe, I am very poore . . .
> and if now I haue a desire to mend, and being in so good a
> way, you know how uncharitable it were in you to put me out
> of it. You may make an honest man of me, if it please you; and

when thou hast made me one, by my troth Mall Ile keep
myself, for I am a gentleman by the fathers side and the
mothers side. (I, p. 329)

Marriage and financial dealing are fluid enough sources
of both seriousness and humour, but the one constant and un-
parodied element in this is the idea of gentlemanly birth. Under
the circumstances, Lady Ramsie, and, one presumes, the audience, cannot fail to be charmed rather than offended by John's
openness; she drinks to John Gresham's health, gives him a gift
of twenty pounds and pays his creditors. The scene ends with
John Gresham planning to get rich on the money Lady Ramsie
has donated:

> And if I can grow rich by the helpe of this,
> Ile say I rose by Lady Ramseys kiss.
> > (I, p. 332)

The final couplet suggests a comic tale which is at odds with the
moral and ideological structure of citizen values but at the same
time celebrates the rise of the witty trickster, the comic source of
Heywood's drama.

If You Know Not Me You Know Nobody, like so many of Heywood's plays, is a ragbag of different plots and styles which
completely fails to resolve the contradictions between the
citizen's values of profit and good works, and the comic dynamic
of the trickster plot. The method of writing allows these
contradictions to emerge as Heywood draws eclectically on the
full range of source material from which his plays are made,
ending the play by reverting to the historical events surrounding
the Armada. There is a tiny thread of connection between the
Armada action and the rest of the play in that the queen comes
to open the Royal Exchange and encounters Hobson who had
lent her £100, but for the most part the episode is simply part of
the accumulation of events attaching the city's wealth to the
nation's glory.

The structural incoherence of *If You Know Not Me*, its failure to
conform to a structural logic of character, motive and action has
left the play in a theatrical limbo, unperformed on the modern
stage. By contrast, Dekker's *The Shoemaker's Holiday* achieved

much greater structural coherence by marrying his tale of citizen ascendancy to a narrative of romance. The narrative scaffolding provided by the plot of Simon Eyre's rise to fame and fortune, a citizen myth like that of Gresham and the Royal Exchange, was subordinated to another kind of romance in the low-life love story of Rafe and Jane and the romance between Lacy and Rose.

Perhaps because of this marriage of citizen ideals with romantic plotting, *The Shoemaker's Holiday* is the most critically successful of Dekker's works. In it lies the claim to Dekker's humane mildness, celebrated by critics.[9] More recently, radical criticism, less comfortable with citizen values, has drawn attention to its ideological dissonances. But above all, its narrative strengths and the individuality of its central characters have kept the play on the twentieth-century stage. Yet it is also very much a play whose effects depend upon Dekker's adaptations of the conventions of professional theatre dramaturgy. The opening scene in which Rafe is sent away to fight offers an alternative version of prentice heroism to that offered by the opening sequence of *The Four Prentices of London*. For Heywood's aristocratic prentices, the wars offer the chance of glory, the vindication of their honour; in Dekker's version, conscription is to be feared and the good master, Simon Eyre, tries to buy his prentice out of the muster. When his appeal fails, Simon Eyre, too, invokes the honour of the gentlemen shoemakers but that is set against the reality of war, dramatised by the silent weeping figure of Rafe's wife Jane. Wars and musters are organised by great men and a poor prentice has only the consolation of the good fellowship offered by his workmates who offer him small gifts of money at their parting. Dekker fills out the muster scene with indications of characters and relationships in Eyre's impatience at his wife and his loquacious self-importance created by nonsensical set phrases. Rafe's emotional farewell to his wife also lays the seeds of the plot when he gives her the shoes which will bring them together in the end. The scene has the simple dramatic excitement of a noisy procession: 'Sound drumme, enter Lord Maior, Lincolne, Lacy, Askew, Dodger, and souldiers, They passe ouer the stage, Rafe falles in amongest them, Firke and the rest cry farewel, &c and so Exeunt' (I, i, 234 SD).

Behind the excitement of the muster scene lies the tension of the competitiveness between Lincoln and the Lord Mayor which

provides the drive for the main love story of Lacy and Rose, set
up in the following two scenes. The plot builds on a simple new
comedy situation of young lovers thwarted by mercenary elders,
with the local setting and interest of a contest between aristocrats
and craftsmen. Lincoln clearly tells his nephew

> I would not haue you cast an amorous eie
> Upon so meane a proiect, as the loue
> Of a gay wanton painted cittizen
>
> (I, i, 75–8)

but, later in the play, the Lord Mayor and Simon Eyre agree that
the traditions of guildsmen constitute as important a lineage as
any aristocracy. However, social conflict is resolved by comedy.
The citizen's fear of aristocratic profligacy is allayed by Lacy's
ability to work as a craftsman and a shoemaker; Rose's citizen
origins are unimportant compared with the faithfulness of her
love!

In order to dramatise his young lovers, Dekker reaches for the
most conventional poetic tropes. Rose appears *'alone, making a
Garland'* which she can then describe and Lacy, in his soliloquy,
explains his disguise 'like a Dutch Shooe-maker' by invoking the
commonplace of Ovidian metamorphosis. The two soliloquies
are standard poetic fare; what provides their life is the appearance of Sibil, Rose's maid with her comic scepticism about Lacy,
and in Lacy's case, his engagement with the low-life energy of
the shoemaker's shop.

The dramatic energy of the comic exchanges between Simon
Eyre and his workmen allow the scenes in the shoemaker's shop
to act as symbolic locus of harmony in the play. When Lacy
applies for work, the real antagonism between native and foreign
workers is forgotten in the warmth with which he is welcomed
by his fellow journeymen. Work is presented as a mythologised
list of tools, 'a good rubbing pinne, a good stopper, a good
dresser &c' and relations between masters and journeymen in
the exchange of food and jokes, and good humour.

Similarly, the somewhat dubious transactions by which Eyre
makes his fortune are glossed over by his simple appearance in
the emblematic clothing of his rising status. It is enough for Eyre
to put on an alderman's gown to complete the deal with the

Dutch skipper, and though his journeymen mock his pretension, the magical quality of fine clothes is endorsed by their physical dramatic impact and the action which they produce. The stage directions 'Enter Simon Eire wearing a gold chaine' (III, ii, 127 SD) or 'his wife in a French hood' (III, iii, SD) chart his progress through the action and act as a countervailing movement to the certainty of his values, summed up in his catchphrase, 'prince am I none, yet am I princely born'.

The one false note in this simple dramatic structure is provided by the figure of Hammon. He first makes love to Rose, acting as a complication in the Rose/Lacy love story and then turns his attentions to Jane who has inexplicably left the shoemakers and waits for Rafe's return alone. In the scene where Hammon is introduced, we can see Dekker, once again, reverting to commonplace dramatic structures to fill out the scene of their meeting. The setting is a hunt in which Hammon comes upon Rose and Sybil by accident which allows the dramatist to pad out the scene with playful courtship in the *double entendre* of hunting metaphors arranged in elegant, if conventional, couplets. This dramatic style cannot convey the threat Hammon poses to the potential comic conclusion and in the following act he is easily dispatched when Rose refuses to marry him and he turns his attention to the 'wench keepes a shop in the old change' (III, i, 50).

The simple functionality of Hammon's role in the play prevents him from offering any real alternative to either Lacy or Rafe as lovers. His contemptuous dismissal of courtly love behaviour (III, i, 40–7) remind the audience where Rose's true affections lie, but there is no serious dramatic opposition of values at work since Lacy has proved himself by taking on the shoemaker's role. Similarly, when Hammon woos Jane the conventional structure of the scene and the poetry makes it impossible to characterise him as an intrinsically evil man. Dekker gives the encounter between Hammon and Jane, dramatic excitement with the familiar structure of the 'looking on' scene used by Heywood in *Edward IV*, when the king woos Jane Shore:[10] 'Enter Iane in a Semsters shop working, and Hamond muffled at another doore, he stands aloofe' (III, v, SD). His soliloquy of passion, by drawing on convention, confuses our attitude to him. He is the wrong lover for Jane in the story

but his passion is expressed in terms which are usually the
marks of sympathetic devotion:

> thus oft haue I stood,
> In frostie euenings, a light burning by her,
> Enduring biting cold, only to eie her,
> One only looke hath seem'd as rich to me
> As a king's crowne, such is loue's lunacie
>   (III, iv, 15–19)

Hammon seems less sympathetic when he moves from en-
quiring the price of Jane's wares to the price of her hand, but he
then insists that his love is chaste, acknowledges her love for her
husband and only wants to marry her when he reveals that her
husband is dead. There is no evidence to suggest that the false
information about Rafe's death is given in anything but good
faith for consistency of character is always subordinated to the
demands of a particular scene. The audience knows that Rafe has
returned and the function of the scene is to increase the suspense
and prolong the action.

Dekker's great skill in the play lies in the excitement of the
finale. Lacy and Rose go off to marry in secret, her father and
Lincoln are tricked into going to the wrong church and Jane is
rescued by the jolly shoemakers as she is on her way to marry
Hammon. In that scene the potential for violence and the simple
contrast between true love and commerce only add to the scene's
excitement. The scene opens with the journeymen *'and fiue or sixe
shoomakers, all with cudgels, or such weapons'* (V, ii, SD) and there
is a dramatic confrontation between the shoemakers and Hammon with his servants. Jane is placed between them as the prize
in the men's conflict. Of course, she chooses her husband and
when Hammon offers twenty pounds for her hand, it provides
Rafe with the opportunity for a stirring speech asserting his
unmercenary values: 'Sirra *Hammon Hammon,* dost thou thinke a
Shooe-maker is so base, to bee a bawde to his owne wife for
commoditie, take thy golde, choake with it, were I not lame, I
would make thee eate thy words' (V, ii, 81–4). Hammon immediately repents his offer, gives Jane the money for her dowry and
the crisis is resolved in order to prepare for the harmonious
finale in which the king himself asserts the transcendant values

of true love, approves all the matches and joins in the Lord Mayor's feast.

It is difficult to read the ideological significance of *The Shoemaker's Holiday*. The action and the speeches touch on the real opposition between merchants and aristocrats, and the impotence of ordinary working men, but those problems are resolved in the story of true love, the assertion of absolute values of good fellowship and the brotherhood of men. The pleasures of wit and wordplay, and narrative excitement, unite the audience in endorsing those values but they do so in the explicitly mythologised world of the golden age of earlier times. There is a darker side to the play in Hammon's opportunism, in Rafe's wounding, in the violence which lies beneath the shoemakers' solidarity. It can be, and has been, brought out in modern productions but the play's structure and the triumph of comedy also address the audience, not only as citizens but as part of a mythologised humanist ideal. It is impossible to tell with what degree of cynicism or sentimentality the audience, both in the public theatre and at court, responded to this appeal in 1599. It was to be treated very differently in the division of the audience and the fragmentation of the theatre profession in the new century.

By the turn of the century, citizen values of the kind celebrated by Dekker and Heywood, were mocked by the witty dramatists who wrote for the re-established boy player companies. In Jonson, Chapman and Marston's *Eastward Ho*, the honest trades-man Touchstone with his catchphrase 'work upon that now' is a parody of both Hobson and Simon Eyre. In other plays, the accumulation of wealth and pride in citizen status is reduced to cheating and sharp practice.[11] In *If This Be Not a Good Play the Devil is in It*, Dekker, too, offered a more satirical view of London's commercial world in a plot where the merchant Barter-vile is visited by the devil. The devil encourages Bartervile's villainy in order to ensure his damnation and the action exposes the corrupt opportunism of his commercial affairs. The Bartervile scenes show Dekker drawing on traditional complaint material (often from his own satiric pamphlets) and using the simplest devices to turn it into dramatic action.

Act II, ii introduces Bartervile's establishment with a stage direction:

> A Table is set out by young fellowes like Merchants men,
> Bookes of Accounts upon it, small Deskes to write upon, they
> sit down to write Tickets. (II, ii, SD)

The detail of the setting provides an air of authenticity but it is
also capable of being generalised into a representative model of
city practice. The 'young fellowes like Merchants' have no role
in the action and like those who later 'to and fro bring in Bags,
and haue Bills' (II, ii, 15 SD) they are there to set a scene in the
manner of an emblem. A 'Bravo' enters 'with money' which
provides the opportunity for a rehearsal of satiric commonplaces
against whoring gallants and the rival trade in tobacco.

The main action of the scene involves exposing Bartervile's
sharp practice in cheating out of his mortgage a creditor who has
come to redeem his debts. There is a certain comic energy in
Bartervile's desperation as he tries to put off the moment when
the money will be paid. The comedy of Hobson's exchange with
John Tawnie coat is now being used in a more sinister context.
However, the scene lacks any originality. As Hoy notes,[12] Dekker
had described a similar device in the story of the usurer in *The
Raven's Almanack* and almost the same stratagem is used in the
usurer plot of Thomas Lodge's play *A Looking Glass for London
and England*. The point is not to expose a particular vice or
satirise a new danger but to reiterate a moral commonplace in
familiar theatrical terms.

Moral commonplaces about corrupt city practice, however,
are simply the reversal of true citizen values. One of the funniest
but most sympathetic portrayals of the good citizen comes in the
sub-plot of *The Honest Whore*, written with Middleton (a boy
player dramatist) for the Prince's Men at the Fortune. The play
is sub-titled 'The Humours of the Patient Man and the Longing
Wife' and presents a shrew-taming tale, involving a citizen
draper whose patience infuriates his wife and makes gallants
compete to enrage him and bet on the results. Candido's reaction
to their insulting and provocative behaviour is comic in its
extremes:[13] he goes to the Senate dressed in a carpet when his
wife will not release the keys to fetch his gown, and when he
finds his prentice dressed in his clothes, simply puts on
prentice's apparell himself. He is even prepared to tolerate the

flirtation set up to annoy him by his wife and her brother in disguise.

Candido's behaviour shows no concern for the traditional marks of status and identity among citizens, but throughout his trials he holds to the patient application of the principles of honest trading. When an arrogant gallant asks for a pennyworth of material taken from the middle of a bolt of expensive lawn, he replies

> We are set heere to please all customers,
> Their humours and their fancies: – offend none:
> We get by many if we leese by one. . . .
> A pennyworth serues him, and mongst trades tis found
> Deny a pennorth, it may crosse a pound.
>
> (I, v, 121–3; 126–7)

However, the character of Candido is not simply a return to the figures of Hobson and Simon Eyre. The world of *The Honest Whore* is not that of *The Shoemaker's Holiday*. Candido is able to remain patient because he recognises the conflict with gallants for what it is, and eventually the vain and foolish courtiers become the butt of the comedy themselves. Candido's ability to turn the courtiers jests upon themselves gives him considerable theatrical presence, as well as moral strength. When one makes off with his silver gilt beaker, Candido calmly asks his servant to 'Hye to the Constable', confident in the support he can claim from civic authority. The new social order of commerce supported by civic power is better protected against gallant aggressions in which *amour propre* is disguised as honour.

The scenes do involve some comic violence, but Candido is never its instigator. When his brother-in-law comes to taunt him by flirting with his wife, the prentices beat him of their own accord; and when he hires bullies to revenge him, they beat Candido but the apprentices rescue him before he can come to any harm. In the boy player comedy, the comic conflict between age and youth was transferred to the class conflict between respectable citizens and young men about town. When gallant is set against citizen in the popular theatres, the apprentices side with their masters, offering an idealised view of the solidarity among masters and men in the world of trade.

Dekker makes clear that this was as much a matter of theatrical style as it was of social observation. When Candido is tormented by his wife's flirting, he tells his brother-in-law firmly

> Trust me, you are not wise, in mine own house;
> And to my face to play the Anticke thus:
> If youle needs play the madman, choose a stage
> Of lesser compasse, where few eyes may note
> Your actions errour; but if still you misse,
> As heere you doe, for one clap, ten will hisse.
>   (III, i, 58–63)

The lines make sense in the context, but they are also an unmistakable metatheatrical reference to the boy player stages. They are designed to flatter the sensibilities of the public theatre audience and to identify them with Candido's integrity as well as with his sense of humour.

Dekker's ability to transfer the ideas and imagery from the boy player companies to the Fortune and the Red Bull complicates the simple opposition often made between their tastes and styles. As we have seen, Dekker presented himself as writing across the divide between popular and élite culture, and the location of satire was part of the negotiation involved. In *The Whore of Babylon*, Plaine Dealing, who informs the Queen about low-life in the city, denounces satirists saying that

> some of them in places as big as this, and before a thousand people, rip up the bowels of vice in such a beastly manner, that (like women at an Execution, that can endure to see men quartered aliue) the beholders learne more villany then they knew before. (II, i, 109–14)

In his amphitheatre plays, Dekker's satire, whether of merchants or of citizen wives, carried no such danger. It revealed in the most old fashioned of dramaturgy that usurers are wicked, not because they lend money at interest but because they prevent the honest from regaining their own. Gallants who mock and trick an honest tradesman are discomfited but the conflict between merchant and consumer, the problems of a market can all be resolved by good fellowship and patience. Such views endorsed a populist solidarity against the sharpers and tricksters, and those who tried to make good against the law.

II

Dekker's commitment to old-fashioned values and styles of popular entertainment was also evident in the speeches he contributed to the pageants prepared for the king at his coronation entry into London. These pageants for royal entries and for the Lord Mayors of London were a kind of street theatre in which an audience of citizens were entertained both with the panoply of the procession and with speeches and allegorical shows. They were not fully dramatic in form[14] but instead used representations of allegorical emblems and devices. Dekker's contribution to the royal entry of King James in 1603 consisted of three pageants, the Nova Felix Arabia arch at Cheapside which identified James with the phoenix, the Rustic Arch, where James was addressed by Sylvanus, a figure from Elizabethan pageantry, and the New World Arch which presented 'some inchanted Castle' where the king encountered Astrea (Iustice), Arete (Vertue) and Fortuna.

The devices which Dekker used were familiar from the style of pageants which had been used in Elizabeth's time. Elizabeth had often been identified with the mythological figure of Astrea; Sylvanus had appeared before Elizabeth during her progresses to Kenilworth and Elvetham; and the device of the phoenix, expressly identified James with Elizabeth new-risen. Dekker's political point in connecting James with Elizabeth was an unmistakable plea for continuity with the past and it was reinforced in the attention he gave in his pamphlet account of the festivities to the pageants prepared by the Italian and Dutch communities in London. The speeches for the Dutch pageant,[15] in particular, emphasised their status as religious refugees: 'a Nation banisht from own Cradles; yet nourcde and brought up in the tender boosome of Princely Mother Eliza', promising James that 'The Loue, which wee once dedicated to her (as a Mother) doubly doo wee vow it to you, our Soueraigne, and Father; intreating wee may be sheltered under your winges now, as then under hers' (694-9).

However, the gap between these ideals and the political reality of the event is all too evident. By insisting on the continuity of Protestant internationalism, Dekker may have displeased more influential groups at the festivity than he pleased. The Dutch were as much the rivals as the allies of city merchants, and as David Riggs has shown 'these images had no particular relevance to James's plans for the future, nor did they signify any lasting transformation of the state'.[16]

Dekker's account of *The Magnificent Entertainment* allows the tensions between the different groups and the difficulty of uniting them into a coherent audience to appear. His description of the effort which went into building the pageants creates an impression of a whole city united in effort. When the day of the entry comes, the physical fabric of the city becomes its populace:

> The streets seemde to be paued with men: Stalles in stead of rich wares were set out with children, open Casements fild vp with women. All Glasse windowes taken downe, but in their places sparkeled so many eyes, that had it not bene the day, the light which reflected from them, was sufficient to haue made one: (179–84)

However, the actual capacity of that audience to comprehend the full meaning of the events and symbols put before it was more in doubt. Dekker dismisses the learned controversy over the iconography of the figures he describes. In what may have been a side swipe at Jonson, he refused 'to make a false flourish here with the borrowed weapons of all the old Maisters of the noble Science of Poesie . . . (only to shew how nimbly we can carve up the whole messe of the Poets)' (55–8) and forlornly concludes, 'The multitude is now to be our Audience, whose heads would miserably runne a wooll-gathering, if we doo but offer to breake them with hard words' (65–8).

Nor, it seems, were Dekker's poetical devices fully approved by the organisers of the pageant. The song which was performed at the Nova Felix Arabia arch claimed that Troynovant (the ancient name for London) had been transformed by James's arrival from a city to a 'Sommer Arbour' and a 'Bridall Chamber' in which 'Brittaine till now nere kept a Holiday' (883–912). In the text of the entertainment, Dekker urges the reader not to

> let the scrue of any wresting comment upon these words. . . . Enforce the Authors inuention away from his own cleare, straight, and harmlesse meaning . . . that London (to doo honour to this day, wherein springs up all her happiness) beeing rauished with unutterable ioyes, makes no account (for the present) of her ancient title, to be called a Citie, (because that during these tryumphes, shee puts off her formall habite of Trade and Commerce, treading euen Thrift it selfe under foote,) but now becomes a Reueller and a Courtier. (914–24)

Even a temporary denial of the city's particular function and prerogative could have unfortunate political implications when addressed to a king, and Dekker felt it necessary to offer the apology because 'some (to whose setled iudgement and author-itie the censure of these Deuises was referred,) brought (though not bitterly) the life of those lines into question' (933–5).

In the final scene of the first part of *If You Know Not Me You Know Nobody*, Heywood had re-enacted the royal entry of Queen Elizabeth when, famously, she had accepted a bible from a child, affirming her commitment to the reformed religion. At the end of *The Shoemaker's Holiday*, King Henry V had feasted with the shoemakers. In the political world of 1603, the reality was more complicated. The planned opening pageant was cancelled since James did not enter the city from Bishopsgate and the whole event was curtailed because of James's impatience with the speeches so that 'a great part . . . were left unspoken' (1622–4). The hopes for a population united in festivity, which had lain behind the address to the popular audience in the theatre were not and could not be realised.

When Charles came to the throne in 1625, he cancelled his coronation pageant completely. However, the regular street pageants for the annual entry of the Lord Mayor continued, and both Dekker and Heywood were employed to write speeches for them later in the century. Even these quintessentially city events, however, cannot be regarded sentimentally as events which overcame the deep divisions of status and wealth which existed in seventeenth-century London. As Michael Berlin has described, the institution of the Lord Mayor's pageant involved a conscious substitution of official city ceremonial for the more popular festivities associated with May Day:

> The subsequent change in the calendar of civic celebration away from festivals such as midsummer towards the extravaganzas of the Lord Mayor's show at the end of October represented an important shift in the arrangement of the year, a disruption of the pre-Reformation cycle of observances . . . the emphasis in London, exemplified in the urbanity of the Lord Mayor's shows, stressed the secular and privatised values of civic honour and pecuniary worth rather than the structural integration of contending social groups within communities. The early dominance of the mercantile élite in London mitigated the need felt in other towns to perform ceremonies which publicly integrated the various parts of the whole.[17]

Berlin's argument is supported by the evidence of Dekker and Heywood's pageants. The iconography of the main shows and the importance of the speeches rehearsed the values of a mercantile élite, making them, rather than the populace as a whole, responsible for the perpetuation of the virtues of justice and mercy and good government. Nevertheless, the status of the ruling élite had continually to be argued for. The dedication of the printed text of Heywood's 1631 pageant *Londons Ius Honorarium* in honour of George Whitmore of the Haberdashers, asserted:

> More faire and famous it is to be made than to be borne Noble, for that Honour is to be most Honored, which is purchast by merrit, not crept into by descent. (IV, p. 265)

and London's own speech to the Lord Mayor repeats Dekker's image of the city made up of its people:

> my numerous Children round
> Incompasse me? so that no place is found
> In all my large streets empty? My issue spred
> In number more then stone whereon they tread.

To see my Temples, Houses, even all places,
With people covered, as if Tyled with faces.
(IV, p. 275)

Acknowledging the presence of the popular audience sometimes proved a volatile element in the pageants' political meaning. For the most part, the dangers which the incoming Lord Mayor had to avoid were vaguely emblematic. In his *Troia Nova Triumphans* of 1612, Dekker reused the conflict between Envy and Vertue and the representation of Fame from the Magnificent Entertainment of 1603; in 1631, George Whitmore, from the Haberdashers Company was addressed by Ulysses, representing 'a wise and discreet Magistrate', who had just negotiated the passage between Scylla and Charybdis. However, in *Britannia's Honour* of 1628, the incoming Lord Mayor is explicitly advised by the figure of London to

Lop off Disorders, Factions, Mutiny,
And Murmurations against those sit high
(IV, pp. 242–3)

These lines may point to a particular political problem; equally they arise as an obvious extension of the imagery of the emblematic tree, representing the twelve livery companies which was the visual component of this part of the show.

One of the most dramatic of Dekker's shows, the Ironmongers scene in *London's Tempe*, demonstrated the dangers of the most conventional of images when they are given dramatic life and lose their static, allegorical meanings. In a pageant celebrating a member of the Ironmongers' company, a scene in Vulcan's forge showing his smiths at work was an obvious motif to use and 'As the Smiths are at worke, they sing in praise of Iron, the Anvile and Hammer: by the concordant stroakes and soundes of which, Tuballcayne became the first inventor of Musicke' (152–5). However, when Jove addresses the smiths his language slides from celebration to the conventions of satire:

For Vices (mountain-like) in blacke heapes rize,
My sinewes crack to fell them: – Ideot pride
Stalkes upon stiltes, – Ambition, by her side,

Climbing to catch Starres, breakes her necke it'h fall,
The Gallant Roares, – Roarers drinke oathes and gall,
The Beggar curses, – Avarice eates gold
Yet ne'er is fild, – Learning's a wrangling scold,
Warre has a Fatall hand, – Peace, whorish Eyes,
Shall not Ioue, beate downe such Impieties?

(211–19)

The list of vices is abstract enough not to cause particular offence
except that they are those traditionally associated with aristo-
cractic licence and idleness. Dekker seems, as in his pamphlets,
to be urging his audience to engage on a moral crusade and by
implication to associate the new Lord Mayor with it. It may have
been enough to disrupt the sense of harmony and issue a moral
and political challenge to the new civic authorities.

Heywood, for his part, placed the popular audience at more
of a distance from the political meaning of his pageants. They
may have enjoyed the excitement of the shows on water and
land, the atmosphere of general holiday, but their response in the
pageant was seen in a very special way. Heywood's 1637
pageant, *London's Mirror*, acknowledged their presence by including a show which

consisteth of Anticke gesticulations, dances and other Mim-
icke postures, devised onely for the vulgar, who are better
delighted with that which pleaseth the eye, than contenteth
the eare in which we imitate Custome, which always carrieth
with it excuse: neither are they altogether to be vilified by the
most supercilious, and censorious, especially in such a conflu-
ence, where all Degrees, Ages and Sexes are assembled, every
of them looking to bee presented with some fancy or other,
according to their expectations and humours.

By 1637, the divisions in the commercial theatre audience were
well established and though all degrees were welcome at these
city events, Heywood assumed that each would require different
fare.

It was a far cry from the unity of purpose between aristocrats
and citizens offered by *The Four Prentices of London*. The mythologised opposition between the two degrees of society still had

ideological force and Dekker's and Heywood's pageants and plays exposed the divisions as well as attempting to create the appealing fantasy of a unity between them

In his magisterial account of early modern culture, Louis B. Wright asserted that

> In no other dramatist, unless occasionally in Dekker, is the London life of the substantial bourgeoisie so well and so favourably mirrored as in Heywood. . . .
>
> Of all the dramatists who drew material from the life around them Thomas Heywood was the most significant of the stage spokesmen of burgher ethics and ideas . . . he sets forth a doctrine of thrift, industry and fair play.[18]

However, both the 'burgher ethics' and the dramatic forms available to represent them were under too great a pressure to be simply celebrated. The thrust towards comedy and satire, the needs of dramatic narrative render that representation both more complex and more interesting.

4
Women and Dramatic Form

I

Dekker and Heywood's prentice plays and city pageants created a dramatic form in which the relations between commercial and civic virtues are negotiated by men; women appear only as the icons of virtue (Lady Ramsey, Mercy, Justice and so on) on whose behalf and in whose name the negotiations take place. The history plays, too, dealt with the public, male world of politics and rebellion but the presence of the queens extended the action to the world of women and, as we have seen, turned politics into emotion through their sympathy with Elizabeth's feminine appeal. A significant number of Dekker's and Heywood's plays similarly focus on women and their role in these narratives, together with the way in which they are represented, create new possibilities for the style and emotional appeal of the drama. These plays significantly shaped the genres of the popular stage and explicitly addressed an audience which included, and came to be defined, by the inclusion of women.

In *Sir Thomas Wyatt*, for example, the sad story of the brief reign and early execution of Lady Jane Grey provided a generalised leitmotif of pathos against which to set the more dangerous emotions aroused by political rebellion. Sympathy for

Lady Jane, of course, had political resonances. She was promoted as successor to Edward VI in order to pre-empt the accession of the Catholic Mary Tudor and, as told by Foxe, her story involved a thorny political conflict between loyalty to religion and loyalty to a rightful monarch.[1]

Dekker and his collaborators emphasised the sense in which Jane and her beloved, Lord Guilford Dudley were the victims of their more politic fathers. They are always reluctant monarchs; as Jane protests to her husband:

> Troth, I doe inioy a Kingdome having thee
> And so my paine be prosperous in that,
> What care I though a Sheep-cote be my Palace
> Or fairest roofe of honour.
>
> (I, ii, 5–8)

The politics of rebellion are neutralised into an antithesis between worldly ambition and the transience of earthly glory expressed in terms which could be echoed by every member of the audience who is aware of the distance between commoners and kings. Jane asks her father 'was your Fathers Father/Ere a King?' and wishes that she 'might still continue of his lyne/Not travell in the cloudes'.

In equating kingship with the simple operations of primo-geniture, Jane bypasses the vexed political problems of the Tudor line and the question of allegiance to a popish tyrant which informs Foxe's version of the story. She is able to do so coherently since she and Guilford act primarily as chorus to the affairs of great men. From their vantage in the Tower, they describe the crowd gathering for Mary's coronation 'As if prepared for a tragedie', eliding the tragedy of Suffolk's death with the larger tragedy (as Foxe saw it) of the reign of bloody Mary.

This tragedy is, of course, also their own and it is given theatrical life in the lengthy final scene of the lovers' trial and execution. Jane and Dudley display their lack of ambition and their love for one another which is set against the evident injustice of the prosecution's claim that they 'manifestly adorned yourselves with states of Garland imperiall'. They accept the technical validity of the charge of treason, but their eloquent defence draws on an iconography of good and evil which has no bearing on the points of law:

> We sought no Kingdome, we desired no Crowne
> It was imposed upon us by constraint
> Like goulden fruit hung on a barren Tree,
> And will you count such forcement treacherie.
>
> (V, i, 69–2)

Jane in particular becomes an emblem of the pathetic transience of earthly glory. Before her execution, she slowly removes her clothes, stressing the symbolism of her action in the accompanying speech:

> Off with these robes, O teare them from my side,
> Such silken covers are the guilt of pride.
> Insteed of gownes, my coverture be earth,
> My worldly death for new Celestiall bearth.
>
> (V, ii, 131–4)

In a grotesque final sequence, Jane's severed head becomes itself an emblem of innocence as Guilford invites the audience to contemplate its

> ruddie lippe, a cleere reflecting eye
> Cheekes purer then the Maiden oreant pearle.
>
> (V, ii, 164–5)

Where Foxe had presented Jane and Guilford as the first victims of a popish queen, this text, without denying that reading of the action, also offered as theatrical pleasures the affecting or grotesque stage image, together with the familiar poetic resonances of the transience of earthly things.

The old-fashioned dramatic style in which Lady Jane's story is presented to some extent disguises the radical dramatic shift involved in the transformation of history into melodrama. A number of recent feminist critics have described how, at different historical periods, questions to do with women, the world of domesticity and emotional life re-emerge at different periods in the resurgence of melodramatic form.[2] A similar process seems to be at work in the construction of early modern theatre of which Dekker and Heywood were a part. The role of women and the extension of the subject matter of the drama into the domestic realm were explicitly addressed in the anonymous *A Warning for Fair Women*, whose Induction offered truthful reportage as an explicit alternative to the tragedy of revenge. In the contest between the popular genres of Comedy, History and Tragedy, Comedy dismissed the conventions of revenge tragedy, set at court and dealing with

> How some damn'd tyrant to obtain a crown
> Stabs, hangs, impoisons, smothers, cutteth throats:
> And then a Chorus, too, comes howling in
> And tells us of the worrying of a cat:
> Then, too, a filthy whining ghost,
> Lapt in some foul sheet, or a leather pilch,
> Comes screaming like a pig half stick'd,
> And cries, Vindicta! – Revenge, Revenge!
>
> (ll. 43–50)[3]

This was no abstract discussion of artistic theory but a contest over theatrical styles. Tragedy defended the appeal of his art for audiences, insisting on an alternative to the conventions of revenge in the tears which the true events of the story brought forth.

The tension between true reportage and the need to set a moral example was difficult to achieve in the theatre. The writer, in effect, separated the two into parallel actions which contrast the true story of Anne Saunder's adultery with a series of allegorical dumb shows depicting the conflict between Lust and Chastity. The allegorical conflict holds the moral framework in place and clarifies the action by providing motivation absent from the main plot, and giving a kind of moral weight to the sometimes trivial and frustrating turns of Browne's attempts to murder Saunders. The author of *A Warning for Fair Women* was only partly successful in resolving the conflict between morality and style, but the Induction indicates the extent to which the question of the representation of domestic life and the concerns of women was a matter of conflict over the tastes of the new audience and the appropriate style in which to present material which addressed their concerns.

These artistic problems are interestingly worked through in Heywood's attempt to combine the stories of usurpation and rebellion in the reign of *Edward IV* with the king's 'loue to faire Mistrisse Shore, her great promotion, fall and miserie, and lastly the lamentable death of both her and her husband' (I, p. 2).[4] In the play's compressed episodic structure, character and motivation are left unexplored but the dramatic impact of individual scenes creates an emblematic contrast between king and commoner which turns on the dramatic significance of the female figure of Jane Shore. As in *A Warning for Fair Women* and in the presentation of Lady Jane in *Sir Thomas Wyatt*, the woman character is used as a visual emblem, her action elaborated in the 'word' of a male onlooker's speech but the opposition between male and female is further complicated by the contrast between king and commoner. The use of physical objects and the setting of the scene where Edward seduces Jane places the action in a citizen world. The prentice enters *'preparing the Goldsmiths Shop with plate'* (p. 63). Mistress Shore comes in *'with her worke in her hand'* and while she *'sits sowing in her shop. Enter the King disguised'*.

His soliloquy both explains his disguise and expresses his wonder at Jane's beauty:

> Oh rare perfection of rich Nature's work!
> Bright twinkling spark of precious diamond,
> Of greater value than all India. . . .
> Her radiant eyes, dejected to the ground,
> Would turn each pebble to a diamond.
>
> (p. 64)

The commonplace images of women's beauty as a jewel[5] can here be extended into the dialogue with the familiar but nonetheless powerful irony of bargaining over a jewel in a shop when the true jewel of chastity is part of the market. The woman character becomes a locus of value but also the focus of emotional appeal. Her figure is a part of the symbolic staging in which Jane is seen by both king and audience, the object of his desire and their narrative attention. The audience shares, quite literally, the king's point of view; the layering of comic disguise with divided stage, and the consistent ironies of imagery and situation produce a complex theatrical effect.[6]

Jane and the king have different senses of what is involved in their sexual exchange and they are also given different language in which to express their perceptions of it. Jane rejects Edward's wooing and when he persists, reminds him of his responsibilities as a king:

> The sunne that should all other vapors dry,
> And guide the world with his most glorious light
> Is muffled up himself in wilful night.
>
> (p. 75)

Edward responds with the language of élite love poetry

> The want of thee, Fair Cinthia, is the cause.
> Spread thou thy silver brightness in the aire
> And straight the gladsome morning will appeare
>
> (p. 76)

The high cultural language of love poetry is presented both as a seduction technique and as a mask for his true sexual intentions which are soon made explicit:

> But leaving this our enigmatick talke,
> Thou must sweete Jane, repaire unto the Court.
>
> (p. 76)

Jane's final seduction is indicated unequivocally in the un-mistakable sign of sexual wrongdoing when her husband's boy reports

> Master, my mistresse, by a nobleman,
> Is sent for to the King, in a close coach.
>
> (p. 78)

Once Jane's seduction is effected, her relationship with the king ceases to be of any interest, but the potential for emotion generated by dramatic ironies is not exhausted. She is presented doing good on the king's behalf, dealing justly with suitors for his support and pardon, and denouncing the merchant who begs

> a licence to transport corne
> From this land and lead to foraigne realmes.
>
> (p. 83)

However, all her good actions are placed in the context of her adultery, for this scene is watched by her husband who glosses the action, contrasting her new role as influential courtesan with her former status as chaste city wife. The contrast is made both in his speech and through the dramatic significance of her clothes. The stage direction describes her as '*lady-like attired . . . unpinning her Mask*'; Shore's speech underlines the moral point, describing how

> now she goes deckt in her courtly robes.
> This is not she, that once in seemly blacke
> Was the chaste sober wife of Matthew Shore.
>
> (p. 82)

The stage directions chart the emotional movement of the action as '*She espies her husband, walking aloof off, and takes him for another Sutor*' (p. 83), and then '*Here she knowes him, and lamenting, comes to him*' (p. 84). There follows a duet of regret for time past and the conflict between honour which is owed to a king and the honour of faithful marriage:

> Therefore, sweet Jane farewell, once thou wast mine;
> Too rich for me; and that King Edward knew
> Adieu, O world, he shall deceived be,
> That puts his trust in women or in thee.
>
> (p. 85)

The story of Matthew Shore and his wife provides an alternative view of the loyalty of citizens, stressing the emotional costs of allegiance to the king which are glossed over in the active scenes of their support against the usurping bastard Falconbridge. It contrasts royal honour with the honour of citizens which rests upon the domestic virtues of chastity and conjugal fidelity. These virtues are, of course, terribly fragile because they depend on women. The woman character, as a result, always carries particular symbolic weight. Her actions are watched over by her husband as they had been by the king, and then men interpret her behaviour in their speeches. She is also, of course, viewed by the audience so that she is both the object of the male characters' desire and the audience's narrative attention.

In the second part of the play, this domestic focus is transferred to the king himself in the scene where Jane Shore is taken to see the queen whom she has wronged. She fears revenge but in these plays women deal in the melodramatic actions of tears and sympathy. At the climax of the scene, the action takes place in dumb show as the queen *'draws forth a knife, and making as though she meant to spoile her face, runs to her, and falling on her knees, embraces and kisses her, casting away the knife'* (I, p. 129). When Edward returns, expecting conflict, the scene is once more resolved in dumb show: *'As Jane kneels on one side the King, so the Queene steps and kneeles on the other'* (p. 131).

Edward's dilemma is given no further dramatic attention for the action soon moves to his death and the accession of Richard III. Jane's role is then given its most powerful emotional appeal as she becomes the central dramatic focus for King Richard's tyranny. He banishes her for her adulterous connection with the former king and she appears, transformed by another set of clothes, *'in a white sheet barefooted with her hair abour her eares, and in her hand a waxe taper'* (I, p. 165). She remains on stage for several scenes and the fate of all the remaining characters in the play become connected with hers, their virtue or villainy determined by whether they relieve her or scorn her fate. Heywood is thus able to draw the different plots of the previous actions together. The comic figures, Jockie and Jeffrey save her from starvation. They comically pretend to play at bowls with *'cheese and halfpenny loaves'* which they bowl towards her; she is relieved by Brakenburie when he can no longer suffer Richard's tyranny, and by Aire whose pardon she had obtained from Edward IV. At every stage she speaks the laments for their suffering, drawing the moral conclusion with the authority which comes from her own experience of suffering. The final sequence shows Heywood's characteristic style:

> Jockie *is led to whipping over the stage, speaking some words but of*
> *no importance. Then is young* Aire *brought forth to execution by the*
> *Sherriff and Officers, Mistress* Shore *weeping, and master* Shore
> *standing by.* (p. 180)

The clown playing Jockie is allowed to ad lib his suffering, but
the rest of the characters are given eloquent set pieces in which
their sense of loss and their memory of the past both create
pathos and draw the plot-lines together. By the end of the scene
the physical arrangement in which they put '*the body of yong* Aire
into a Coffin . . . and then he sits down on the one side of it, and she
on the other' (I, p. 183) sums up the story of Jane's adultery, her
repentant good works and her final suffering. Shore who appeared to her on numerous previous occasions, both in and out
of disguise, once more forgives her and their final duet builds up
the pathos:

> O dying marriage! oh, sweet married death
> Thou grave which only shouldst part faithful friends
> Bringst us togither, and dost joine our hands.
> O living death! even in this dying life,
> Yet ere I go, once Matthew kiss thy wife.
> *He kisseth her, and she dies.*
>
> (I, p. 183)

The emotional power of the scenes with Jane and Matthew
Shore indicate the new dimensions which a woman character
provided for the popular drama. She extended the action into the
arena of men's sexual honour but also provided the drama with
a direct emotional dimension with which to engage the audience, a sense that the drama could deal with their day-to-day
existence. The iconography of clothes, the emotional emphasis
on loss and the irrecoverable nature of domestic happiness
provided a dramatic language which transformed history into
melodrama. It displaced the politics of tyranny into an action
which focused on sexual intrigue but also involved personal
honour and domestic happiness, concerns which could be shared
directly by the audience in the theatre. The figures of women
(played on stage by boys) were both the signs of sexuality,
observed and constructed as such by men, and exemplars of the

consequences of deviant behaviour. But these sexual narratives elicited emotional responses which offered the pleasures of pathos and suspense, as well as endorsing citizen morality.

II

In *Edward IV*, Heywood used the role of Jane Shore to transform history into domestic melodrama. Jane's virtuous use of her power as Edward's courtesan and her brave resistance to Richard's tyranny created a new kind of dramatic emotion in the ironic tension between accepted moral values and the dramatic pleasures of pathos and emotional involvement. This new dramatic style found its greatest fulfilment in Heywood's masterpiece, *A Woman Killed with Kindess*.[7] The play replaced the framing action of royalty and rebellion with a provincial setting, creating the sense of a real community grappling with social and personal problems. The contrasting stories of an adulterous wife and a woman who used marriage to save her brother's fortunes are dramatised through a telling combination of realistic detail and powerful poetry, which gives a density to the commonplace emotions expressed.

The music and dancing of the opening scene, for example, create a realistic sense of the life of a country community and also act as symbols of the harmony which the ensuing action will destroy (see I, i, 69–70). A use of detail which is both realistic and symbolic is evident at all the key moments of the action. When Wendoll seduces Anne with inexplicable ease and Nick the faithful servant informs his master, the possible confrontation is withheld while the whole house-party plays at cards. The commentary about which game to play and who will play false creates ironies which work at both a symbolic and a narrative level. The familiar trope of sex and games is given dramatic life by the realistic details of the setting. The scene opens with a procession of servants from dinner: '*one with a voider and wooden knife to take away all, another the salt and bread, another the table cloth and napkins, another the carpet*' (III, ii, SD). Master Frankford then enters 'brushing the crumbs from his clothes with a napkin, as newly risen from supper' and before the game of cards is played 'They spread a carpet, set down lights and cards'. The apparently

naturalist action is used to set up dramatic ironies which
generate both the suspense and the sense of loss which are
crucial to the tragic conclusion.

A similarly subtle use of emblematic and mimetic staging is
used in the scene where Frankford discovers the adulterous
lovers; it skilfully balances outrage at the lovers' behaviour, with
sympathy for Frankford's loss. The lovers are kept off-stage,
keeping the focus on Frankford's point of view, which can then
hold the moral and emotional reaction in tension. He describes
how:

> I have found them lying
> Close in each other's arms, and fast asleep.
> But that I would not damn two precious souls
> Bought with my Saviour's blood and send them laden
> With all their scarlet sins upon their backs
> Unto a fearful Judgement, their two lives
> Had met upon my rapier.
>
> (XIII, 42–8)

This speech emphasises the pathos of his situation which is
increased by his lament on the inexorable passing of time. The
wish

> that I might take her
> As spotless as an angel in my arms.
> (XIII, 61–2)

invokes the lost happiness of the beginning of the play,
insulating the sense of his loss from any consideration of his
wife's or her lover's feelings.

Having achieved this measure of control over the audience's
emotional attention, the text then packs the remainder of the
action into dumb show: '*Enter* WENDOLL, *running over the stage in
a night gown, he* [Frankford] *after him with his sword drawn; the
Maid in her smock stays his hand and clasps hold on him. He pauses
awhile.*' As Alan Dessen has pointed out,[8] the maid's action is
perfectly integrated into the realist mode of the action but it
creates a stage picture which carries all the symbolic meaning of
the allegorical actions of psychomachia, inherited from an earlier

dramatic tradition. Frankford makes the connection plain in the speech which acts as the 'word' to this dramatic emblem.

> I thank thee, maid; thou like the angel's hand
> Hast stay'd me from a bloody sacrifice.
> Go villain, and my wrongs sit on thy soul
> As heavy as this grief doth upon mine.
>   (XIII, 68–71)

Frankford is both mankind, saved from mortal sin by an angel, and a particular human figure, grief-stricken by his wife's adultery.

Anne's role in the play, like Jane Grey's and Jane Shore's, is to act as the emblem on which the tragic action is played out. As Frankford says, her actions only exist to bring out his reaction

> Spare thou thy tears, for I will weep for thee
> And keep thy countenance, for I'll blush for thee.
>   (XIII, 84–5)

She is instantly remorseful and Frankford's 'kindness' in banishing rather than killing her allows the play to draw out the tragedy of his situation in the sorrow of hers. He lists all she has lost; then he calls for her children and immediately sends them away lest

> her adult'rous breath may blast their spirits
> With her infectious thoughts.
>   (XIII, 126–7)

At this point Anne addresses the women of the audience directly, urging them to see her as exemplary, warning that

> when you tread awry,
> Your sins like mine will on your conscience lie.
>   (XIII, 143–4)

The direct debt to the dramatic form of morality plays is evident, but the dramatic impact is far more powerful and, in being linked to Anne's masochistic call for a physical punishment which would redeem her honour, more complex.

Frankford's dual role as judge and tragic hero depends upon a tense relationship between the symbolic and mimetic force of this style of drama. As domestic melodrama, the play provides a role for men which is different from the heroism or rebellion they displayed in the history plays. Frankford, like Matthew Shore, can be the focus for emotional sympathy which does not depend on the trope of the fall of great men, but at the same time he is distanced from a purely domestic role. In the scene after Anne's banishment, he moves through the house removing all visible traces of her life there, and comes across her lute. The scene stops as he soliloquises on the instrument, remembering its former harmony, symbolic of the harmony of their marriage. However, he hardens his heart and sends Nicholas to return it to her. It is a complex moment whose effect depends entirely upon performance. It could be played for pathos with the audience empathising with Frankford's loss, but it could equally act as a reminder of the dangers of domesticity and the trap of emotion for men.

In the remainder of the play, Anne, like Jane Shore, plays on the audience's emotions. Nicholas brings her the lute, and the action stops while she plays on it. With her lute she stands both as an image of the seductive woman and as an icon of lamenting womanhood, while the other stage figures act as a controlling chorus. Wendoll appears, to speak of recognition and lament, and even Nicholas joins in with the other servants' tears:

> Why how now, eyes? what now? what's here to do?
> I am gone, or I shall straight turn baby too.
>
> (XVI, 67–8)

In the final scene, Frankford forgives Anne on her deathbed. It is a scene of immense pathos, created by the ironies of restoration at the moment of greatest loss. Frankford is given the Christ-like power of forgiveness. He is also given the social power to restore to his wife the 'lost names' of 'wife, the mother to my pretty babes'. The appropriate response to this action, the balance between moral awareness and human sympathy is made explicit by Anne's neighbour, Sir Francis at her deathbed:

> I came to chide you, but my words of hate
> Are turn'd to pity and compassionate grief;
> I came to rate you, but my brawls, you see,
> Melt into tears, and I must weep by thee.
>
> (XVII, 63–6)

The contrasting action of Susan Mountford in the sub-plot also presents the ways in which, although men's social power controls women's fates, their honour, family and kin were all mediated through women. Susan's brother is imprisoned because of his debts to Sir Charles and tells her that she can save the honour of his house by becoming his whore. He is concerned to keep intact the 'virgin title' of his honour 'never yet deflowered' but urges Susan to give up the rich jewel of her chastity for his debts. Susan refuses to do so and the plot is only resolved when Sir Charles agrees to marry her. Conventional pieties remain unscathed and Susan's feelings are not investigated. As a whole, the play's emotional dynamic depended less on the creation of individual characters than on creating a general sense of the precariousness of happy marriage and the enormous emotional investment which it involved.

This preoccupation with marriage in the plays of the turn of the century, suggests a concern with changing social relations between men and women which many critics have connected to a real historical crisis in the organisation and control of marriage, both in local communities and the state.[9] This real historical concern fed into the rivalries between dramatic companies as they competed for the attention of new audiences with plays that addressed concerns and reflected lives of domestication rather than courtly romance. However, narratives centring on marriage and sexual relations also created new aesthetic opportunities for the dramatists.[10] Mary Beth Rose has shown how marriage as an ending gave coherence to the diverse forms of romance; dramas of adultery, like *A Woman Killed with Kindness*, extended the form further by creating a narrative movement in which happy marriage is threatened and the action can play on the drama of loss. In *A Woman Killed with Kindness*, Heywood adapted emblematic actions to a realistic scenario which dramatised key moments in a marriage moving from harmony to disruption and loss. He may have been responsible for another Worcester's Men play where the marriage action provided a looser scaffolding for a wider variety of dramatic entertainments.

In *How to Tell a Good Wife from a Bad*, the title encapsulates the proverbial problem of marriage, polarising women into good and bad wives with little opportunity for doubt about which was which. The good wife of the play, Mistress Arthur is (like Anne Frankford)

> loyal, constant, loving, chaste:
> Obedient, apt to please, loath to displease:
> Careful to live, chary of her good name,
> And jealous of your reputation.[11]

On this occasion, however, it is not her chastity that is besieged but her husband's unexplored lack of love for her which leads him to abandon her, woo another and finally attempt her murder. This narrative of abuse, however, is only the flimsiest scaffold for a series of comic turns. There is a running gag of an old man who constantly contradicts himself by agreeing with whatever his companion says, a comic Justice ignorant of the law, and schoolroom scene involving jokes in dog Latin. Even Mistress Arthur's death is dramatised by her clownish servant beating up his friend in his excess of grief, and when the officers come to arrest the murdering husband, the dramatist cannot resist a comic set piece in which each officer cowers behind the other, reluctant to enter the fray.

Mistress Arthur's brave despair at her husband's cruelty and her faithful support for him even in his villainy are affectingly written but they too are *set pieces* inviting amazement rather than understanding. There is a passing suggestion early in the play that the couple were married too young but this engagement with the real social issues of marriage is lost in the simple opposition between the good wife, all perfection, and the wicked courtesan Mary with whom the husband becomes infatuated. Mary, in turn is given a set piece with her bawd and her comic servant which establishes her wickedness, and there is no surprise but some humour in the scene after she marries Master Arthur when she and her bawd make it clear that even though married, she 'will have her will'.

The audience is reassured that the basic social structure of marriage remains in place while the social problems of erring husbands and unruly women are acted out in the safe context of firmly-established moral and social norms. The dramatic potential of an adulterous woman is for pathos and horror; the adulterous man is not condoned but his action can as easily be turned to comedy while the unruly woman varies the action in her comic contrast to the perfect wife.

III

Narratives of marriage and adultery which could evoke both comedy and pathos offered dramatic building-blocks which proved a vital resource in the rapid turnover of play production. In *Patient Grissil*, for example, Dekker, Chettle and Haughton each took different angles on marriage to contribute to the variety and diversity of a threefold action. The main plot involves the testing of wifely obedience when an aristocrat marries a peasant; the play also includes the contrasting stories of a shrewish wife and one who resists marriage altogether. These contrasting narratives of marriage offered a range of dramatic pleasures and the scope for a variety of different styles. The Grissil story provided scenes which could dramatise the politics of base marriage, reverting to a recurring theme of earlier romantic comedy.[12] The opening scene presents a courtly discussion of marriage and love which elegantly turns the hunting scene in which it is located, into a source of imagery for a disquisition on the longing and beauty, sighs and sweetness of love.[13] The following scene indicates the shift to a lower social milieu partly by the stage direction which shows Grissil and her father entering '*with two baskets*' and partly by the costumes, the 'grey gowne for gryssel' which was recorded in the payments for the play.[14] The change of social setting also involves a change of style in the comic monologue from Babulo, the clown. Like Shakespeare, Dekker was to integrate his clowns into characters, giving Babulo the task of mediating sympathy for Grissil and keeping a common-sense reaction to the events. However in this scene he produces the nonsensical filling monologue which only creates instant laughs and good humour with well-worn jokes and catch-phrases.

The scene also shows a creative interplay between realistic detail – Janicle's references to the weather – and such formal emblematic elements as the mood-setting song 'Art thou poore, yet hast thou golden Slumbers' (I, ii, 93–111). The same combination is evident in the prolonged scene where the Marquis asks Grissil to chose between him and his courtly companions: it is a judgement of Paris in reverse and a test of the courtiers who try to avoid being chosen without insulting Grissil or the Marquis's choice of her for his wife.[15] The action is then compressed into the Marquis's acceptance of Grissil which provides the story of their loves couched in the poetic oppositions between wealth and virtue, beauty and love.

Chettle and Dekker apparently wrote the Marquis/Grissil plot between them[16] but the play is also padded out with the contrasting comic action of the reverse kind of marriage between Sir Owen and Gwenthyan. The opening scenes of this plot present standard comic fare in making the rivals for Gwenthyan's hand a country knight who speaks affectedly, and Sir Owen whose thick Welsh accent and bellicose country manners may have caused hilarity in a metropolitan audience, especially when accompanied by his servant Rice, a clown with the tic of eating secretly and choking as he speaks.

These dramatic types can generate any number of comic set pieces, such as Emulo's description of his duel with Sir Owen in which the main victims were his clothes. This sort of description was part of the comic repertory of the braggart soldier from *commedia dell'arte* and Haughton indicated that the actor could continue it extempore if it was amusing the audience.[17] The dramatist thus indicating the extent to which the play was made out of available dramatic material which relied upon the interaction of collaborating dramatists and experienced players. A similar set of comic tropes inform the scenes in which Sir Owen tries to gain some control in his marriage. Gwenthyan's Welsh railing depends on the cumulative comic effect of repetition and is only loosely structured by the recurring quarrels about her extravagance. The important source of conflict in marriage is submerged in physical comic effects: Sir Owen angrily tears up her rebatoes; Gwenthyan tears up his five-thousand-ducket bond in retaliation; the whole scene ends in anarchy as they both then turn on the unfortunate servant Rice.

The play's dramatic fare is completed by the interchanges between Julia and her suitors whose witty style is taken from romantic comedy. Julia is given all the arguments against marriage from the praise of virginity 'that makes us saints on earthe and starres in heaven' (II, i, 264), the indictment of marriage as 'a battle of love' and the folly of waiting on Cupid. The arguments are put, not as the opinion of a coherent character (though she could become that in a certain style of performance), but as an element in an argument, a residue of dramatic tropes from the comic materials inherited by Dekker and his collaborators.

Conventional oppositions between different kinds of women provided simple contrasts with which to vary the ways in which women characters provided dramatic resources for the stage. They also explored the ideology of marriage and the changing relations between men and women which it involved. The story of Patient Grissil involved a Marquis who marries a peasant. He transforms her into a lady but when her children are born he takes them from her and returns her to her father. She bears his cruelty with fortitude and is rewarded when he invites her back to court for his remarriage, only to reveal that the bride is her child. Her reward for patience is to be reinstated as Gwalter's wife with the love and blessing of her children. Chaucer's clerk who told the story in *The Canterbury Tales* presented it as one of exemplary patience in the certainty of Christ's mercy. Its later revivals, in a ballad and in a dramatic version by John Phillips,[18] show the social meanings superseding the allegorical. In her account of the development of Elizabethan comedy, Mary Beth Rose has described how sexual love provided a cohering narrative for romance material, offering what she calls an 'erotic teleology' which can provide closure in marriage.[19] The dramatists could have taken the well-worn path of resolution in marriage, beginning with the Marquis entering disguised to Grissil and taking the action to the consummation of their love: making more of the rivalry between Sir Owen and Sir Emulo, or forcing Iulia to choose among her suitors. However, this story compresses the mechanics of the love narrative, shifting the focus to the regulation of marriage itself. By Act II, ii, the

Marquess confides his plans to test Grissil's obedience to his courtier, Furio. Knowledge of the plan reassures the audience that he is in control of the ultimate happy ending but does nothing to mitigate the violence of the following scenes. They use the style of domestic tragedy in which the woman on stage is the focus of sympathy, but they also allow both the dramatist and the audience to indulge in the sadistic imagery of tragic misogyny in a comfortable comic context. Grissil acts as the ideal of wifely concern, offering to 'beare/The burden of all sorrowes, of all woe' when she encounters her husband's unexpected anger. But these domestic virtues cannot assuage his anguish at the way his public position has been compromised by his base marriage, crying

> I hate thee more then poyson
> That stickes upon the aires infected winges,
> Exhald up by the hot breath of the Sunne,
> Tis for thy sake that speckled infamie,
> Sits like a screech-owle on my honoured brest,
> To make my subjects stare and mocke at mee. . . .
> Thinkst thou then I can loue thee (oh my soule)
> Why didst thou builde this mountaine of my shame,
> Why lie my ioyes buried in Grissils name?
>
> (II, ii, 50–61)

The audience shares and sympathises with Grissil's astonishment in the change of her lord's attitude, but they are also offered a pleasing display of the high-flown rhetoric taken and adapted from a different dramatic context. Chaste and obedient, Grissil is being denounced like an adulteress and the dramatic excitement as in Matthew Shore's or Frankford's loving forgiveness of their, in fact adulterous, wives is created by the unexpected and emotionally-charged reversal of the appropriate response. In these domestic plays, the woman's role shifts from being a function of the narrative, a sounding board for male ideology and becomes an alternative focus of sympathy, undermining male authority.

Dekker's and Heywood's innovations in domestic drama bring new theatrical potential into the repertory available to other playwrights. The Marquis's rejection of Grissil is echoed by

Shakespeare's more controlled use of this dramatic effect in
Othello, and the sexually-charged moment in *The Changeling*,
when Beatrice refuses to accept her fallen glove from the hands
of Deflores, is also prefigured in Dekker's play. Furio offers the
Marquis his glove and instead, the Marquis orders Grissil to
stoop for it. She readily obeys and he then forces her, while on
her knees, to tie Furio's shoes. In an aside, he admires his wife's
constant patience so that in the same dramatic moment, the
audience can experience the Marquis's total control of Grissil's
body, itself a fantasy of male ideology, his admiration for her
virtue, and horror that it should be so arbitrarily exercised.

This double vision also permits some space for a subversive
view of the power relations of patriarchy. The Marquis taunts
Grissil by reminding her of her former poverty. In a telling use
of the symbolism of physical effects, he hangs up her old clothes,
her 'russet gentrie, coate and crest'. Grissil's acceptance of the
intended insult, however, undermines it by acknowledging her
human integrity when she says

> Ile cast this gaynesse of, and be content
> To weare this russet braverie of my owne,
> For thats more warme then this, I shall looke olde,
> No sooner in course freeze then cloth of golde.
>
> (II, ii, 73–6)

The scene both looks back to the emblematic use of clothes in the
presentation of Jane Shore and forward to Lear's reminder to
Regan

> If only to go warm were gorgeous
> Why nature needs not what thou gorgeous wear'st
> Which scarcely keeps thee warm.
>
> (*King Lear*, II, iv, 267–9)

Grissil's speech dramatises the personal pride in her sense
that her human worth does not depend on the Marquis's favours
or the clothes he offers. It is a pride shared by her humble family.
When the Marquis banishes them from court, he reminds them
too of her old clothes. Babulo the clown defiantly asserts 'Grissil
was as pretty a Grissil in the one as in the other'. When the

Marquis contemptuously reminds them to take away her waterpot, he again insists 'many a good messe of water grewell has that yeeled us'.

As a presentation of a coherent character, the Marquis's actions make no sense. There is a critical gulf between the Marquis's behaviour to Grissil and the soliloquies in which he deplores his courtiers' flattery, generalises it to a view of the world and plans for her safety. The scenes are not driven by a sense of character so much as a juxtaposition of dramatic effects drawn from the conventions for representing marriages in crisis.

This dramatic style dealt in strong and varied emotions which are particularly powerfully invoked in the scene where Grissil's babies are taken from her. Grissil is at her most pathetic but also at her most female and the tension between her obedience to her husband and her natural maternal instincts is explicitly invoked. She insists that she alone must nurse them:

> I pray thee let them suck, I am most meete
> To play their Nurse: theyle smile and say tis sweet,
> Which streames from hence, if thou dost beare them hence,
> My angrie breasts wil swell, and as mine eyes
> Lets fall salt drops, with these white Necter teares,
> They will be mixt: this sweet will then be brine,
> They'll crie, Ile chide and say the sinne is thine.
>
> (IV, i, 129–35)

As the good courtier Furio sums up 'I thinke my Lord shee's a true woman, for she loues her children, a rare wife, for shee loues you . . . and I thinke shee's more then a woman, because shee conqueres all wrongs by patience' (IV, i, 213). It is a scene where the origin of the dramatic effects involves considerable risk for the coherence of the play. The Marquis, in spite of his explanatory asides, is put in the position of Herod in the plays of the Massacre of the Innocents, instructing his flatterers to tear Grissil's babes from her and denouncing them as 'a loade of shame/Of speckled shame' (IV, i, 60–1). The 'natural' and emotionally-approved reaction to children is seen in the loving behaviour of Grissil's father and Babulo. They are given an extended scene (IV, ii) of untrammelled sentimentality which includes the lovely lullaby, 'Golden slumbers kisse your eyes' and suggests a natural affinity between love for children and the spontaneous response of ordinary folk.

The varied sources of the play's dramatic devices threaten not only the consistency of characters but also the consistency of its argument about women. Grissil is not only contrasted with Gwenthyan the shrew, but with the evil flatterers who support the Marquis's tyranny. Her total obedience is lavishly praised as exemplary, wifely behaviour but the same total devotion to the Marquis's will is condemned when shown by his sycophantic courtiers. Total submission to a ruler is presented as base and dangerous flattery, and the play offers examples of a robust resistance in the role of Grissil's university-educated brother, Laureo. He is quick to denounce the Marquis both when he is banished from the court and when Grissil is sent home. The possibility of resistance to aristocratic tyranny is both hinted at and denied in the scene where Furio comes to take the children away. He is intercepted by the Marquis himself, disguised as a fellow basket-maker. He tries to rescue the babies, crying 'The Marquesse is a tyrant and does wrong' (IV, ii, 170) and is eagerly supported by Babulo who responds like the prentices of the city comedies with 'O rare, cry prentises and clubs . . . sirra set down thy baskets and to't pell mell' (IV, ii, 166–7).

A similar strand of resistance is evident in the Owen/ Gwenthyan plot when she invites the beggars in to eat the banquet which she has been expected to prepare for the Marquis. This scene provides an opportunity for rowdy horseplay as '*they quarrell and grow drunke, and pocket up the meate*' (IV, iii, 39 SD).

but the speeches offset any explicit sense of insubordination by including 'God Save the Duke' several times amid the beggar's rambling. A hint of chaos lurks at the edges of the drama, suggesting a threat of social chaos in the world outside. More importantly, it indicates that if Gwenthyan is controlled by violence she will behave violently and not be held to the ordered hospitable functions of a wife. Gwenthyan acts throughout as a sceptical commentator on Grissil's forbearance. At the end, the comic conclusion is held in place by her plea that her violence had been to test Sir Owen and she would be more reasonable in future. However, the warning remains 'good Knight be not proude and triumph too much and treade her Latie downe, God udge mee will tag her will again doe what her can' (V, ii, 268–70).

It has become commonplace to treat this version of the Grissil story as an intervention in the sexual politics of early modern England,[20] discussing how far the play indicates the dramatists' attitudes to women and marriage. The discussion turns on how far Grissil's patience exemplifies the ideal advocated by the writers of Puritan handbooks on marriage and how far an audience's attitude to it is modified by the comic portrayal of the alternatives offered by Gwenthyan and Julia. The sense of potential chaos just beyond the action and the more explicit engagement with the issues of popular politics allowed the possibility of theatrical pleasures offering an alternative view of the ostensible morality of the narrative. However, the theatrical pleasures of pathos and comedy work within a wider context in which women, whether patient or shrewish, are ultimately controlled by men and only have dramatic life as the objects of male control. Grissil in particular behaves as the Marquis's puppet, dressed by him as great lady or simple peasant, and behaving as he desires. Her virtue rests in her obedience as his wife and vassal, the bearer of his children, but that virtue can as easily be rejected when he transfers her obeisance to Furio, or as easily takes away the children which he gave. Julia, to be sure, resists the blandishments of her various suitors but she too exists only as the object of their desires and even while resisting marriage has no alternative life which she can choose, or even alternative affections which she can express.

It is difficult to draw large conclusions about early modern marriage from plays which are so evidently determined by working through familiar theatrical permutations. However, in placing women at the centre of their plays and focusing their actions on marriage, Dekker and Heywood extended the emotional and dramatic range of the theatre in which they worked. They provided a context in which the concerns of ordinary people were given a dramatic voice and in which the theatre could deal with the theatrical pleasures of pathos and sympathy which were often in tension with received morality. The women characters, to a large extent, retained their emblematic force as images of good or evil, determined by their clothes, viewed and commented on by men, but the dramatists also extended the possibilities of dramatic form by contrasting comedy with pathos as potential styles for women characters contributing to the range and variety of theatrical pleasures afforded by the stage.

5
The Challenge to the Popular Stage

I

As the theatre developed in the more competitive climate of the new century, the representations of domestic life seem to have offered more than just an alternative style in drama; they seem to have played some role in forging the social identity of the popular audience and the significance of women within it. The representation of women and low-life characters challenging the authority of their social superiors was endorsed by the emotional and theatrical impact of the ways in which their stories were dramatised on the stage. Unusual corroboration of this phenomenon was provided by Christopher Brooke in his *Ghost of Richard III* (1614). He suggested that the exemplary function of displaying women's sexual misdemeanours was outweighed by the pathos which it invoked. His Richard comments

> And what a piece of Iustice did I shew
> On Mistress Shore? when (with a fained hate
> To unchast Life) I forced her to goe
> Bare-foote, on penance, with deiected state?

But now her Fame by a vild Play doth grow:
Whose Fate, the Women so commiserate,
That who (to see my Iustice on that Sinner)
Drinks not her Teares; and makes her Fast, their dinner?[1]

This evidence about the response of women in the audience to stories of adulterous melodrama suggests that moral censure was being mitigated by commiseration.

In the new theatrical styles of the turn of the century, this melodramatic sympathy for the adulterous woman, associated with ignorant women's taste was contested by a vogue for satiric misogyny. The new writers for the boy players of the indoor theatres created a theatre which addressed its audience as a sophisticated élite, confident of its urbane values, appreciating drama which mocked and parodied the styles of the older popular theatres. They mocked the sentimental approach to women as they had parodied citizen values. The story of Jane Shore was explicitly repudiated in the description of a popular audience 'of Civill Throats stretchd out so lowd' who 'Came to see Shore or Pericles'.[2] Beaumont in particular sneered at citizen women's taste for exemplary narratives in *The Knight of the Burning Pestle*. His citizen's wife, the antithesis of his desired new audience, had never been to the theatre before 'but I should have seene Jane Shore once and my husband hath promised me any time this Twelvemoneth to carry me to *The Bold Beauchams*'[3] (Induction, ll. 51–3). The taste for domestic melodrama was rejected as old-fashioned in spite of the contemporaneity of many of the plays, and was considered suitable for the tastes of women ignorant of the latest theatrical fashion.

In denigrating popular culture through its association with the tastes of women, the fashionable writers began a tradition which continues to this day.[4] However, the contest to establish a separate form for élite drama was complicated by the involvement of some of the same dramatists in the different theatrical contexts. The shift to satiric misogyny was, moreover, only one of the many variations in the dramatic potential of stories about women. Heywood had adapted history plays to melodrama and in *Patient Grissil*, Dekker and his collaborators had challenged the courtly styles of romance with a domesticated narrative of marriage. Dekker's *Westward Ho*, written with Webster for Paul's

Boys, shifted the treatment of sexual material once again, offering a new satiric style in which the threat to marriage is presented as comic, less a matter of pathos and regret than a matter of trickery and wit. The theatrical pleasures it offers are not those of moral certainty but of witty games and the power to see through role-playing and affectation, distinguishing gallant from gull rather than good from evil. Wit in these plays is less a matter of verbal dexterity than a set of social attitudes which endorses the style and behaviour of the 'witty young masters of the inns of court' who were its targeted audience. Dekker's and Webster's play subjects the domestic world to urbane criticism, informed by the commonplaces of misogynist satire. Marriage is under threat once more, but the play is located in the world of citizen women whose determination to have their will, like mistress Mary in *How to Tell a Good Wife from a Bad*, is now accepted as comic and is part of a contest between the women and the young gentlemen who attempt to exploit them.

Westward Ho offers the delicious illusion of a private view of women's vice in which the humour comes from simply displaying the wives' arch raillery as they offer mocking summaries of their husbands' and lovers' failings. This familiar fantasy of women's insubordination is given a particular edge by being placed in an explicitly modern setting. Mistress Honysuckle, for example, talks of 'going to puritan Lectures' and to a banquet and warns Mistress Wafer against breastfeeding her child: 'if a Woman of any markeable face in the Worlde giue her Child sucke, looke how many wrinckles be in the Nipple of her breast, so many will bee in her forheade by that time twelue moneth' (I, ii, 117–20). This is the antithesis of Patient Grissil's concern to nurse her own child. It is the discourse of a world where fashion and style are everything and signals the women's defiant determination to stay in that world rather than conforming to the conventional expectations of chaste silence and obedience.

In their treatment of sexual relations, the play dramatised the world of verse satire but its apparently new 'realism' is a result of taking old devices and exploiting their sexual potential to the full, presenting its audience with an eroticised, rather than romantic or domestic, view of its world. The women's eagerness to learn writing is sexualised in a scene where Iustiano, one of the husbands, comes to see them disguised as a writing master.

The resulting sequence draws on the comic schoolmaster routine familiar from *Love's Labour's Lost* (IV, ii) or *The Merry Wives of Windsor* (IV, i). In the new satiric style, the dreary puns in bawdy dog Latin are transformed into sexual play with the idea of a woman's skill in holding a pen, a *double entendre* which comically escapes the foolish, indulgent husband but is offered up for the audience's enjoyment.

Citizen women are not the only objects of this sexual joking. Their husbands are involved in a scene set in a brothel where, as it turns out, they are all frequent clients. Moral judgements of their behaviour are swamped in laughter as the scene plays out the classic farce of each arrival forcing the previous one to hide until all four husbands are secreted about the stage. Shakespeare had used a similar device in *Love's Labour's Lost* (IV, iii), but where in that play the courtiers are involved in an intrigue of courtly love, the men in *Westward Ho* are buying sex.

The new setting significantly alters the terms in which women and their actions are viewed. In these comic sequences, women's sexuality is presented as completely available for men, both as the subject of bawdy talk, and as desire that can be used or dismissed at will. When Birdlime, the bawd, tells the gallant Master Monopoly that Mistress Tenterhook is love with him, the comedy is all at her expense:

MONOPOLY.   Fewh? pray thee stretch me no more uppon your *Tenterhook*: pox on her? Are there no Pottecaries ith Town to send her Phisick-bils to, but me: Shees not troubled with the greene sicknesse still, Is she?

BIRDLIME.   The yellow Iaundice, as the Doctor tels me: troth shees as good a peat: she is falne away so, that shee's nothing but bare skin and bone: for the Turtle so mournes for you.

MONOPOLY.   In blacke?

BIRDLIME.   In blacke? you shall find both black and blew if you look under her eyes.

MONOPOLY.   Well: sing ouer her ditty when I'me in tune.

(II, ii, 209–19)

Monopoly's arrogance is typical of the gallants' attitude to women's sexuality. This is not simply the attitude of a character placed in the action but part of a special appeal in the way the play addresses its audience. Where in the domestic tragedies the audience were addressed as moral judges,[5] here they are referred to in a number of metatheatrical comments which link the worlds of the audience and the play. In the soliloquy which ends the opening scene, Iustiano asks 'Haue amongst you Citty dames? You that are indeede the fittest, and most proper persons for a Comedy . . .' (I, i, 225). It is not clear if the city dames are appropriate as subject-matter or audience, and elsewhere the young men of the audience are flattered by being presented with a witty mockery of 'A Templer or one of those cogging Cattern pear-coloured-beards, that by their good wils would have no pretty woman scape them' or 'some yong perfum'd beardles Gallant . . . that spits al his braines out ats tongues end' (II, ii, 149–51; 170–71). The flattering attention paid to the audience of just such young men would easily offset the apparent mockery of their style. The play at such moments offers an image of a festive world in which the young and witty have the best lines and the most fun.

In spite of this eroticised humour, the moral focus of the play remains firmly conventional. The city wives accept the gallants' invitation to go 'Westward Ho' with them and their plotting to do so is full of entertaining action. However, the wit with which they deceive their husbands is also used to thwart their lovers and the adultery is never consummated. The comic balance between wit and morality is not fully achieved. The sub-plot which involves the elderly earl's plan to seduce Mrs Iustiano creates problems of consistency of style in which the language of domestic melodrama overlays the comic tone of the rest of the action. Having accepted the bawd's invitation to visit the earl, Mrs Iustiano nevertheless denounces him with all the fervour of outraged chastity. She excuses her visit to the earl as womanly healing 'in pitty of your sick hart', but she claims that pity has caused her to forsake her true self:

> see I cloth'd
> My limbes (thus Player-like) in Rich Attyres,
> Not fitting mine estate, and am come forth.
>
> (II, ii, 108–10)

she then laments her fate in the language of moral abstractions more commonly found in the domestic melodramas

> Pouerty, thou bane of Chastity . . .
>   Oh tis rare
> To finde a woman chast, thats poore and faire.
>   (II, ii, 146–7)

The earl is eventually punished by an elaborate trick: he is courted at a banquet by her husband in disguise and when, appalled, he realises his mistake, is forced to confront both the horror of his action and the corpse of 'Mistress Iustiano as though dead' (IV, ii, 110 SD). He is then denounced before the citizens and acknowledges his guilt.

The problem of consistency is also found in the figure of Iustiano. He is comically involved as the disguised writing master in the plot of planned adultery but in soliloquy deploys the language from a quite different theatrical style. Having helped Mistress Honeysuckle to deceive her husband, He denounces women's 'art / To hood-winke wise men thus' which he has aided and abetted and then offers the audience a conventional misogynistic homily:

> Well, if (as Iuy bout the Elme does twine)
> All wives loue clipping, there no fault in mine.
> But if the world lay speechles euen the dead
> Would rise, and thus cry out from yawning graues,
> Women make men, or Fooles, or Beasts or Slaues.
>   (II, i, 232–6)

Iustiano's rhetoric is inconsistent in the plot of the play but it is in keeping with the men's role as controllers of women's sexuality. The young men's sexual indulgence was witty only when it suited them and their traditional punitive Shrove Tuesday rampage through the brothels of London is celebrated in Master Monopoly's description of how he is 'in an excellent humour to go to a valting house, I wold break downe all their Glass-windowes. hew in peeces all their ioyne stooles, tear silke petticotes, ruffle their periwigges, and spoyle their Painting'

(III, ii, 15–18). Controlling women could be the subject of moralising melodrama or it could be the occasion for a comic romp.

The difference in tone between the scenes with the earl and
the rest of the play may be the result of a difference in taste and
style between Dekker and his young collaborator.[6] However, a
simple opposition between Dekker's conventional morality and
Webster's sexual libertarianism cannot account for the complex
interaction of styles and their relationship to the traditions of the
popular theatre. It is interesting that the earl alone among
the would-be adulterers is punished. He is quite explicitly contrasted with the witty gallants by Birdlime, the bawd, and the
contrast suggests that he violates both the moral and the comic
codes by being both aristocratic and old. When he meets Mistress
Iustiano he is presented, not as a witty young rake but as
an example of the seducing aristocrat seen in Heywood's
Edward IV.[7] In Heywood's play, the king's power was threatening and potentially tragic; here aristocratic power is comically
undercut by Birdlime's sales-pitch for the sexual appeal of citizen
women:

> name you any one thing that your cittizens wife coms short
> of to your Lady. They haue as pure Linnen, as choyce paint-
> ing, loue greene Geese in spring, Mallard and Teale in the fall,
> and Woodcocke in winter. (I, i, 26–9)

The earl's passion for Mistress Iustiano is not the wild oats of
youth but a consuming desire which, again like Edward with
Jane Shore, he glamorises with the high cultural rhetoric of love:

> You giue my loue ill names, It is not lust
> Lawless desires well tempered may seem Iust
> (II, ii, 83–4)

The 'tempering' of his lawless desires takes the form of an
eroticised worship expressed in poetic imagery. He is not playing
with lust but is totally committed to his passion so that

> my Hart
> My Happiness, and State lie at your feet.
> (II, ii, 72–3)

In the world of boy player comedy, such language feels old-fashioned and out of place. The self-deluding, foolish worship of women is treated as comically as cuckolded citizens or overdemanding whores. Conventional morality still has some purchase on the action in the outcome of the plot but the conventions of romance, the aristocrat in love with the low-life girl seems played out as a theatrical convention and can be freely mocked. As a result, the potentially terrifying theatrical *memento mori* in which the audience as well as the earl is confronted by the contrasting images of the banquet of lust and the dead object of that lust is merely another joke. Mistress Iustiano is really alive and the affair is just another witty story:

> the booke of the siedge of *Ostend*, writ by one that dropt in the action, will neuer sell so well, as a report of the siedge between this *Graue*, this wicked elder and thy selfe, an impression of you two, wold away in a May morning.
>
> (IV, ii, 186–9)

Like the boy players work itself, moral (or immoral) stories are grist to the commercial mill. In this market, stories or morality or sex itself are only valid insofar as they will sell. Birdlime makes the connection when she reminds Mrs Iustiano of the market in which she must function:

> A woman when there be roses in her cheekes, Cherries on her lippes, Ciuet on her breath, Iuory in her teeth, Lyllyes in her hand and Lickorish in her heart, why she's like a play. If new, very good company, very good company, but if stale, like old Ieronimo, goe by, go by.   (II, ii, 181–5)

The tension in *Westward Ho* between the new boy player style and the moralising rhetoric of the scenes with the earl suggests that the new style had not fully established its contrasting fashions and the ways it wished to address its assumed new audience. 'Old Ieronimo' had become a byword for old-fashioned drama, but as Dekker's work for both the boy players and the adult theatres showed, it was not so easy to determine appropriate styles when dealing with the questions of sexual relations and sexual morality. The domestic tragedies had

opened up conventional social norms to the display of pathos
which mitigated their severity; the boy players attempted to
eroticise the narratives of wit and trickery in a similar free space
of theatrical pleasure. However, the relationship between pathos
and wit, comedy and morality was never completely resolved.

Westward Ho clearly found its audience. The rival boys
company, the Children of the Revels at Blackfriars produced an
answering play, *Eastward Ho* which was answered in turn, by
Dekker and Webster's *Northward Ho*. In the opening scene, the
gallant Greenshield plans revenge on old Mayberry because the
citizen's wife has refused him through 'puritanicall coynesse'.
However, the action of the play exposes the fantasy at the centre
of the cuckolded citizen plot. Mayberry pretends to assist
Greenshield's plot but instead, enacts a citizen's revenge for a
gallant's slur on his wife's honour. The plot of the virtuous
maligned Mrs Mayberry resolved easily and becomes the spring
for other actions of comic revenge.

Much of the play's theatrical energy comes from scenes of
low-life local colour. References to London locations make up a
discourse of their own which generates puns, plots and
description in which every word has potential *double entendre*.
The play seems a celebration of the excess of London as a source
of energy and comic pleasure. Everything in London is available
for consumption and the role of sexuality in that culture is made
explicitly by Doll the whore who comments 'Siluer is the Kings
stampe, man God's stampe and a woman in man's stampe, wee
are not currant till wee passe from one man to another' (I, ii,
81–3). The wit of the action consists in passing the women
around until one gallant cuckolds another, and is in turn, tricked
into marrying the whore.

In this world of consumer culture, the absolutes of morality
lie not in notions of marital fidelity but in feelings which trans-
cend the exchange of commodities. These feelings are centred on
the poet Bellamont who urges the citizen to believe in his wife's
fidelity, is generously tolerant of his son's misdemeanours and
represents the central integrity which is recognised even by the
prostitute, Doll. She is mystified by her passion for him, finding
that he has none of the attractions she associates with lust,
lacking 'flaxen haire, yellow beard, French doublet, nor Spanish
hose, youth nor personage, rich face nor mony' (IV, i, 153–5).

His witty son attempts to embarrass him and discredit his disapproval of his son's life by setting up an affair between his father and the whore. Bellamont is tricked into visiting her but his discomfiture at being found with a whore by his son is less important than the moral lesson in tolerance and abstinence he teaches him.

The way in which Bellamont thwarts his son's plot, is a model for the action as a whole. All of the disparate actions come together when the whole company leaves London to go to Ware, and each would-be cuckolder finds himself tricked. The basic comic structure of the biter bit is overlaid by a moral structure in which the values of fidelity, tolerance and good humour are presented as fundamental. The wit of citizen comedy is acknowledged and the worldly wisdom of the low-life characters is presented as a corrective to the narrow-minded morality of the citizen women.

II

The complex morality and dramatic styles of Dekker's collaborations with Webster for the boy players offers some indication of the shifting boundaries and interconnections between the private and public theatre plays of the turn of the century. Dekker's and Heywood's domestic dramas had established a role for women characters and a style which was associated with popular drama. This style sat uneasily with the new sophistication of boy player theatre and was self-consciously opposed to the taste for urbane sexual comedy. However, as the same dramatists worked both for the boys' companies and the adults at the old amphitheatres, the new style itself penetrated the public theatre. Dekker's and Heywood's later work for the public theatres shows the influence of new styles of comedy together with a new attitude to sexuality and the ways in which it could be represented.

At the same time as Dekker was writing the Ho plays with Webster for the boy players, he was working with Middleton for the Prince's Men at the Fortune on Part 1 of *The Honest Whore*. Like *Northward Ho*, the play involved a whore thrown into emotional turmoil by an encounter with an honest man. The

appearance of a whore as a central character suggests an attempt
to adapt sophisticated city comedy for the public theatre
audience, though in using the narrative of the 'converted
courtesan',[8] conventional morality was kept firmly in place.

The whore of the title does not appear until the second act
when she is introduced with an elaborate stage direction in
which her man, Roger, lays out the tools of her trade: 'a stoole,
cushin, looking-glasse, and chafing dish . . . a violl with white
cullor in it, and two boxes, one with white, another red painting'
(II, i, SD). This scene-setting is given a measure of theatrical
space in which to establish the brothel scene and the actor takes
equal responsibility for doing so: 'He places all things in order
and a candle by them, singing with ends of old ballads as he
does it. At last Bellafront (as he rubs his cheeke with the cullors)
whistles within' (II, i, SD). As in the scene of Jane Shore's seduction, the physical setting acts both to give a sense of realism to
the stage-world and to indicate a symbolic context for the action.
The physical objects on stage both locate the scene and also
become the symbolic objects for Roger's good-humoured wit
about women's deception which is then enacted as Bellafront
dresses and makes-up on stage.

The scene presents the world of the whore with some charm,
offsetting the bawdy jokes about ruffs and pokers with
Bellafront's songs. The ease with which she inhabits the scene is
carried over into the ensuing encounter with her clients in which
they joke about her various suitors in terms which suggest that
style and sexiness are more significant than social status.
However, this stylish sophistication which creates an easy,
familiar, equality of wit between the whore and the gallants is
challenged by the entrance of Hippolito 'who saluting the
Company as a stranger, walkes off' (II, i, 117 SD). His presence
makes Bellafront increasingly self-conscious as he is sarcastic at
her expense and leaves, evidently impervious to her charm.

This sequence of introduction shows the range of dramatic
possibilities offered by centring the action on a whore. She and
her stage-world can provide an image of the sophisticated con-
sumerist world of the gallant but it also offers a number of plot
possibilities. Hippolito's friend Matheo suggests that meeting
Bellafront will make him unfaithful to the memory of his dead
mistress and when he returns he does flirt with her. However, a

whore also offers the possibility of a powerful range of moral rhetoric. Bellafront tries to win Hippolito with the sad tale of her seduction, sketching in the possibility of a sympathetic response to her, such as was evoked by the tragedy of Jane Shore. However, his angry disbelief builds up into an eloquent denunciation of all whores as the byword for evil, the receptacle of the town filth and the type of political treachery. Characterisation is sacrificed to rhetoric as Bellafront accepts the terms of Hippolito's denunciation and responds with set pieces of complaint in which she accepts that she has become ugly, not merely because of her act of lust but because the action has been named by a virtuous man:

> I am not pleasing, beautifull nor young.
> Hipolito hath spyed some ugly blemish
> Eclipsing all my beauties: I am foule:
> Harlot! I, that's the spot that taynts my soule.
>
> (II, i, 440–3)

This shift from the world of city comedy to the rhetoric of moralising pamphlet literature creates incidental comic effects. When Bellafront's bawd solicits her on behalf of a gentleman that 'smells all of Muske and Amber greece' the whore astonishes her with an unexpected moral denunciation, calling her 'Lusts factor and damnation's orator,/Gossip of Hell'. Bellafront's former lover Matheo is also vilified as

> the first
> Gave money for my soule; you brake the Ice,
> Which after turnd a puddle.
>
> (III, iii, 94–6)

But the recompense of marriage is seen as healing all, as Bellafront regrets that Matheo, in refusing to marry her, will 'love to make us lewd, but never chaste' (III, iii, 120).

The shift in these scenes from easy sophistication to moralising rhetoric indicates something of the tension in the dramatic representation of whoredom. The opening sequence with the gallants has no plot potential. It is merely the local colour, familiar from city comedy. Its potential for action lies only in the possibility of a relationship between the whore and a man, which immediately moves it into a moral world. Nevertheless, the language and imagery of sexuality can provide this play with a good deal of dramatic material. Hippolito's speeches and Bellafront's regrets all take up a good deal of stage-time. In Act IV, i, the play presents a lengthy sequence of Hippolito musing on a skull, reflecting on the transitoriness of human beauty and lamenting the death of Infelice by a generalised reflection on the bare bones scarce hidden by the trappings of life. This merely provides the setting for his encounter with Bellafront who comes to him disguised as a page. She too is repentant, calling on Hippolito to save her soul, arguing that if he fails her she will return to whoring and her sins will be on his head. This opens up the possibility of an awareness of the ways in which men's and women's lust are interconnected but ultimately the blame for sexuality is placed on women. Women are contrasted in purely sexual terms, the simple opposition of lust and chastity. In swearing his vow of eternal chastity in his beloved's memory and in chastising Bellafront, Hippolito uses the full force of theological rhetoric in which women's beauty leads only to the grave – but this is simply the obverse of the gallants' witty acceptance of sexual frailty.

The play's treatment of sexuality as the source both of comedy and moralising, builds on the traditions which Dekker and Middleton could draw on. However, in this scene the two approaches are combined in a most disorientating way. Hippolito's servant produces a constant patter of jokes about men's and women's sexuality and is as amused by Bellafront's cross-dressing as Hippolito is appalled. The effect is partly that the servant's lines are out of control, a case of the clown speaking more than is set down for him; but it also implicitly mocks Hippolito's moralising excess, and places it in a more sophisticated light.

The confusion of bawdy set jokes with a rhetoric of complaint presents opposing moral positions on the role of women and the control of whoredom. However, they also offer contrasting kinds of theatrical pleasure[9] which suggest that the collaborators were exploiting available theatrical resources even at the expense of narrative and thematic consistency. The play begins with the full panoply of a funeral procession which is challenged by

Hippolito who insists that the corpse, his lover Felice, is still alive. His grief is restrained by his friend Matheo who nonetheless mocks his grief with bawdy reminders of the corruptibility of female flesh and the certainty that Hippolito will find immediate solace in a bawdy house.

A number of plots could emerge from such an opening but the action then turns to the sub-plot of the patient citizen Candido and his shrewish wife.[10] Once again, a bawdy undercurrent constantly holds up the dialogue and the encounter between Fustigo and his sister cannot get to the point, for mis-understandings and *double entendres*. When she says that her husband 'haz not all things belonging to a man' her brother assumes his impotence but is corrected by her insistence that she refers to his lack of anger and her plan to have her brother flirt with her to incite her husband's virility.

Both of the plots turn on tricks, for in scene iii, Infelice is revived by a doctor, and we find that her death which caused such anguish to Hippolito is a trick to prevent him from marrying her. The duke's reason is that Hippolito is an enemy, though nobly born and otherwise worthy, and Infelice is, in turn, persuaded that Hippolito is dead. The plotting based on tricks and misunderstandings leaves the loose ends by which it will unravel. The comic or romantic inversion becomes mechanical and so can be solved mechanically.

In the sub-plot, Candido thwarts all the gallants and Fustigo's attempts to rile him and even when he is arrested as a madman (IV, iii), his patient humour does not falter. Without dramatic effort or explanation Candido's wife changes her mind about tormenting him and pleads with the duke to have him removed from the madhouse as she had wished to have him put there. Her suit is overtaken by the news that Hippolito is alive and about to marry Infelice; the duke goes off after him but someone else gets the news to Hippolito first, moving all the actions towards the finale of reconciliation at Bedlam, where Dekker adapts the spatial organisation which he used in the Ho plays to orchestrate the encounters among the different groups.

There is thus a complete separation in the plotting between action and character, and motivation: single-dimensional charac-ters provide variety within a familiar framework. Theatrical pleasures are provided by autonomous set pieces whether the set

piece of Hippolito's denunciation of lust or the more extended
sequence (also used in *Northward Ho*) when the inmates of
Bedlam are displayed and anatomised by their keeper. The
madfolk are brought forward in a series of vignettes in which
each case reflects on the surrounding social world:

> for the Courtier is mad at the Cittizen, the Cittizen is madde
> at the Country man, the shoomaker is mad at the cobler, the
> cobler at the carman, the punke is mad that the Marchants
> wife is no whore, the Marchants wife is mad that punke is so
> common a whore. (V, ii, 145–9)

The structure of estates satire is turned into dramatic emblem
which has no direct connection to plotting but presents extraordinary visual effects such as 'an old man, wrapt in a Net' and
a crazy rhetoric of madness which pushes at the boundaries of
representation. Bellafront has come to Bedlam and is disguised
as a madwoman, but her appearances give an elusive sense of
the real psychological effect of the play's events. The discourses
of the play, held as it is within a rhetoric of conventional
morality, do not allow this to develop, but allowing madness to
speak takes the play both into a surreal realm which has no
connection with reality and at the same time suggest a reality just
beyond the available discourses of the contemporary social
world.

By the end of the play, Bellafront is married to her original
seducer, Matheo, Hippolito is reunited with his beloved,
Candido is reconciled to his wife, and the duke accepts all that
he had formerly resisted. This sense of a barely-controlled
dramatic world makes the machinations of plot seem infinitely
precarious – an imposition of narrative control akin to the social
control imposed by the institution of Bedlam itself.

III

The plotting of *The Honest Whore, Part 1*, the manipulation of
dramatic set pieces and the contrasting social attitudes which
they embodied, offered the possibility of infinite variety. The
dead could come alive, the witty whore be transformed into a

penitent one, and whoredom be translated into a marriage which was as much a narrative as a social solution. By the turn of the century, it was clear that women could be used not only as a vehicles for pathos or moral outrage but as the turning point of plots in which they are the trigger and the solution for dramatic action. Neither whore nor virgin have dramatic potential except as they change their state; virgins in romantic comedy can marry, but in city comedy they must be assailed and whores can either reform or be killed, or exist simply as emblems for set pieces. Married women, too, offer plot possibilities only inasmuch as they deviate from the ideal. They must be involved with adultery, imagined or real, or act as shrews to be tamed or to triumph.

The plot possibilities for women established in Dekker's and Heywood's domestic drama permit a variety of permutations. The characters established by the first part of *The Honest Whore* were accordingly reworked into a second play in which their moral positions were reversed. The penitent whore Bellafront remained penitent but the plot possibilities of her repentance were tested in a further challenge to her honesty together with an additional plot complication in the arrival of her father, acting as a 'prince in disguise' to protect her. The plot of Candido, the patient man from Part I is also reworked and in this play it operates in a kind of shorthand rather than being fully elaborated. Candido has married again, determined on this occasion to control his wife. When this second wife begins to display her bad temper, he is warned and advised by the courtier Lodovico:

What would I have you do? Sweare, swagger, brawle, fling; for fighting its no matter, we ha had knocking Pusses enow already; you know that woman was made of the rib of a man, and that rib was crooked. The Morall of which is, that a man must from his beginnings be crooked to his wife; be you like an Orange to her, let her cut you never so faire, be you sowre as vineger. (I, iii, 109–14)

But then the action is over; as soon as Candido threatens her and here is the prospect of a comic duel with yard and ell (measuring rods in the linen trade), the bride kneels to her husband with a speech of repentance. The scene is familiar from such merry tales as Long Meg of Westminster where a woman's apparent power collapses at the point when she meets a man she can respect.[11]

The stories are varied and the jokes kept alive with the additional pleasure of allowing a knowledgeable audience to build on past plays for the enjoyment of new ones. The formulaic character of the action was clear from the title page of the printed version which offered 'The Humors of the Patient man, the Impatient Wife: The honest Whore perswaded by strong arguments to turne Curtizan . . . and lastly, the Comicall passages of an Italian Bridewell, where the Scaene ends.' The characters are brought on stage in order to display their humours, and narrative is sacrificed in favour of rhetoric whose pleasure lies in its originality. The commonplace denunciation of a whore, for example, is given a devastatingly pointed and original turn in Bellafront's father's memory of her former life which produces his curse 'Were her cold limbes stretch out upon a Beere, I would not sell this durt under my nailes to buy her an houres breath' (I, ii, 162–4). However, this rhetoric is completely unconnected to character for Friscobaldo's role requires that he reveal his 'true' feelings of sympathy for his child, expressed once again in complex imagery, 'She shall drinke of my wealth, as beggars doe of running water, freely, yet neuer know from what Fountaines head it flowes' (I, ii, 171–3) as he prepares to help her in disguise. His disguise involves further swivelling of character and moral position when he engages himself in disguise as Matheo's servant and reviles his own behaviour in order to ingratiate himself and to test Bellafront further.

Just as the set relations between men and women generate plot, so the conventional imagery describing sexual relations can generate further speech. In Act III, i, for example, Friscobaldo and Infelice hold an extended dialogue about her lord's misuse of a park which belongs to another woman. The imagery of park and pale as sexual loci is familiar from the sonneteering analogy between a woman's body and a landscape[12] but it adds nothing to the theatricality of the scene and seems no more than a roundabout way of putting across the simple point of Infelice's unhappiness and Friscobaldo's sympathy. The same metaphoric mode produces an equally-laboured dialogue between Infelice and her husband about whose clock is true or false.

The sources of these images lie in the enormous range of language, tropes and images originating in the formal rhetoric of the quarrel over women[13] Their poetic and theatrical life depended on the variety with which they were used and the extent to which they were reinforced or extended by the dramatic action. In Act IV, i, for example, Hippolito tries to persuade Bellafront to become a whore again 'by the power of Argument' (IV, i, 249). He presents his argument without passion as a rhyming exercise, beginning with the origin of the word Harlot in the name of a 'Concubine to an English King' (IV, i, 263). He exercises the false analogy between sexual and social liberty and works through an extended simile, comparing the whore to the

> Sunne in his gilt Zodiake:
> As bravely does she shine, as fast she's driven,
> But staies not long in any house of Heauen,
> But shifts from Signe, to Signe:
>
>   (IV, i, 281–4)

The connection to character and motive cannot be safely ascertained in this drama of constant reversals but that is less important than the poetic pleasures of analogy and metaphor. Bellafront's speech is also in rhyme and also opens with the familiar rhetorical moves, going back to the beginning of time. However, her argument moves into the pragmatic questions of how a whore is treated:

> so men loue water,
> It serues to wash their hands, but (being once foule)
> The water downe is powred, cast out of doores
> And even of such base use doe men make whores.
>
>   (IV, i, 318–21)

The image's pointed domesticity is part of its pleasure but it is connected like all the other images in Bellafront's speech to a character whose past we know and whose experience in the play extends and tests the imagery of conventional morality.

In Act III, ii, for example, the sleazy underside of gallant affectation is shown in Matheo's maudlin despair at having lost at dice which soon turns into violence against Bellafront. Since his clothes are vital to his status, he takes away hers: 'shall I walke in a Plimouth Cloake, (that's to say) like a rogue, in my hose and doublet, and a crabtree cudgell in my hand, and you swimme in your Sattins?' (III, ii, 32–4). The symbolic disrobing of Grissil which indicated her dependence on her lord, is here turned into a violently realist scene which gives dramatic life to Bellafront's cautious analogy between the cast whore and the cashiered soldier in her speech to Hippolito.

This sense of the economic reality behind the rhetoric of sexual passion and the witty, swaggering style is no more than we would expect from the author of Dekker's prose pamphlets. However, the prose of the pamphlets can only, with difficulty, be extended into dramatic action and Bellafront is the only figure who can achieve this connection between rhetoric and action. When Bots and Mrs Horseleach, for example, lament the lack of flesh available for whoring (III, ii) we can note their rampant commodification of sexuality, but its consequences are left unexamined and the audience is free to respond with moral outrage (like Bellafront) or satiric cynicism (like Lodovico).

The tendency to replace drama with the display of social types is most acute in the finale. As in Part I, all the characters find themselves in a formal institution of social control, Bridewell, where the whores are displayed. The parade of whores is the simplest form of dramaturgy; each whore enters, flanked by the masters of Bridewell carrying the emblems of their oppression 'th'one with a wheele, the other with a blue Gowne . . . one with a blue Gowne, another with Chalke and a Mallet . . . &c' (V, ii, 265, 313 SDs). In this dramatic form, the women are quite literally the object of male scrutiny. They are objects of revulsion but also of intense interest for they offer themselves as emblems of the whole society. Penelope Whore hound, for example, is a whore dressed as a citizen and she complains

if I goe amongst Cittizens wiues they ieere at me: if I goe among the Loose bodied Gownes, they cry a pox on me, because I goe ciuilly attyred, and sweare their trade was a good trade, till such as I am tooke it out of their hands.

(V, ii, 330–4)

Bellafront's claim in her disputation with Hippolito that whores are always identifiable and distinguishable from honest women is borne out. Underlying this certainty, however, is the uneasy suggestion that whoring permeates the whole world of women and the whores cannot be fully identified until they are seen wearing the blue gowns of Bridewell.

The scene in Bridewell is also the context for judging the action as a whole. Matheo is charged with theft, but Bellafront pleads for his life. She is cleared of whoring but only through the agency of Hippolito, and to the very end has to maintain her innocence through her faithfulness to Matheo. Both she and Matheo are finally pardoned by the generosity of Friscobaldo but even his pardon is presented as an unexpected *coup de théâtre*. He seems to be insisting on the duke's justice but then says 'the Law shall haue thy life, what, doest thou hold him? let goe his hand: if thou doest not forsake him, a Fathers everlasting blessing fall upon both your heads' (V, ii, 475–7).

What is at issue is less the morality of deviant behaviour than the right of honest men to sit in judgement. As the Master of Bridewell says

> Some it turns good,
> But (as some men whose hands are once in blood
> Doe in a pride spill more) so some in going hence,
> Are (by being here) lost in more impudence.
>
> (V, ii, 255–8)

Individual attitudes to their sin are less important than the ability of those in authority to exercise that role. The whores' vivid and violent account of how they were 'burnt at fourteene, seuen times whipt, six times carted, nine times duck'd, search'd by some hundred and fifty Constables' (V, ii, 373–5) is rhetorically powerful and suggests a chaos of sexual vice and exploitation. But it is held in place by the Master of Bridewell's complacent account of the effectiveness of the institution in his charge,

offered as a combination of civic pride and reassurance that the
social legislation of Elizabethan London has fulfilled its purpose:

> The sturdy beggar and the lazy Lowne,
> Gets here hard hands, or lac'd Correction.
> The vagabond grows stay'd and learnes to 'bey,
> The Drone is beaten well, and sent away. . . .
> As iron on the Anvill are they laid,
> Not to take blowes alone, but to be made
> And fashioned to some Charitable use.
> Thus wholsom'st Lawes spring from the worst abuse.
>   (V, ii, 37–40, 51–4)

The Master's homily is less theatrically powerful than the
whores' abusive resistance but it invites the audience to share its
point of view and themselves sit in judgement on the action and
the characters. The conventions of the plot and the final resting-
point after the violent swings of the action depends on the
conventions of social critique which can be affirmed, however
precariously, at the play's ending.

The long mad sequence in the Bedlam of Part I offers the
pleasures of wild variety which are held in place by commonplace social observation, such as the automatic satirical
combination of occupational categories and their relations with
women:

> Gafer shoomaker, you puld on my wiuues pumps, and then
> crept into her pantofles: lye there, lye there, – this was her
> Tailer, – you cut out her loose-bodied gowne, and put in a
> yard more than I allowed her, lye there by the shomaker . . .

and then through the series 'Fidler – Doctor – Tayler – Shoomaker. – Shoomaker – Fidler –Doctor – Tayler so! lye with my
wife agen now. . . . '[14] This display of social deviance creates
potentially interesting effects. It is not celebrated as the deviance
of gallant misbehaviour is in the boy player drama, but its
dramatic vitality is in tension with the assured certainty that
social organisation will hold it in control. The audience is being
invited both to supervise this deviant behaviour, like the Master
of Bridewell, but also to see the extent to which it is under

pressure. The moral centre of citizen values is explicitly affirmed, but the dramatic spectacle of the low-life of the city are also part of the play's pleasures.

For those involved throughout the narrative rather than coming to state a moral at the end, resolution seems to depend on coincidence and play-acting. Friscobaldo's disguise serves to expose Matheo and defend Bellafront, and Lodovico disguises himself as a prentice in order to help Candido control his wife. However, the authenticity of their performance either in or out of disguise is always in question since their rhetoric is equally powerful, regardless of the roles they play. Lodovico urges the patient Candido 'to our Comedy, come' (II, ii, 12) and when he claims that he cannot act it, he asks 'cannot you doe as all the world does? Counterfet' (II, ii, 15). Counterfeiting and play-acting which inform the pervasive metatheatricality of the boy player drama also seem to have affected these plays for the public theatre. The plays expose the evils of the town and offer their citizen audience a position of judgement over it. However, they also offer a view in another sense, as the characters display the bewildering range of possible responses, comic, satirical and pathetic to the varied actions made possible by the urban world and the image of it created by the public theatres.

6

The Cross–dressed Heroine

I

The two parts of *The Honest Whore* dramatise the formal and ideological compromises made in Dekker's attempt to conflate the genres of city comedy and domestic melodrama. The representation of women, the theatrical tension between their exemplary function in a moral schema and their roles as the focus of sympathetic identification, was at the heart of this problem but the plays also dramatise the issue of appropriate roles for men in the tension between domestic and city worlds. In the domestic melodramas, the male heroes act as controllers of women, judging their adultery as Frankford does or manipulating their obedience as in the case of Gwalter in *Patient Grissil*. In the comic world of *Westward Ho*, the most attractive men are the witty consumers of commodified sex but they also act as the judges both of the women and of the lustful earl. In *The Honest Whore*, the two functions of consumer and judge are separated. Matheo is partly a witty gallant in the early scenes with Bellafront but his irresponsible consumption of women, clothes and leisure is quite clearly condemned in the second part of the play. Hippolito's moral authority, which allows him to judge Bellafront, is established by his rejection of the pleasures she offers but also by the way he engages with moral abstractions as he muses on a skull (I, IV, i) or manipulates the history and ideology of whoredom (II, IV, i) in order to teach Bellafront and the audience a lesson. The final judgement from the Master of Bridewell and Friscobaldo, Bellafront's father, makes it clear that, whether the setting is domestic or social, men lose none of their patriarchal power. Women can be offered condescending sympathy but their principal role is to offer a new arena for action in which male anxieties about their control of sex in both the domestic and the city world can be dramatised.

The contrasting roles for men and women characters are most successfully resolved in the varied settings of Heywood's *The Wise Woman of Hogsdon*. The play, once again, takes the materials of domestic drama, the 'marriage problem' plot, and places them in a city comedy setting. The seeds of its resolution are transferred from the supervisory men to the heroine disguised as a boy. The play opens on a scene of gallants gambling away their last as the rakish Young Chartley desperately, but comically, tries game after foolish game in an effort to recover his losses. The scene offers the same appeal as the cony catching pamphlets or the manuals of advice, parodied in *The Gull's Hornbook*, which purport to give an informed view of the London scene. However, it also seeks to accommodate the gallants' behaviour and place it within familiar moral norms. The sober Haringfield reminds the gallants and the audience:

> Let's not like debosht fellowes, play our Clothes,
> Belts, Rapiers, nor our needfull ornaments:
> 'Tis childish, not becomming Gentlemen.
> Play was at first ordayn'd to passe the time;
> And sir, you but abuse the use of Play,
> To employ it otherwise.
>
> (I, i, 127–32)[1]

The same sense of a moralised urban world is evident in all the scenes of the first act. Luce, the young citizen, who ends up married to the sober gentleman, signals her virtue, like Grissil and Jane Shore, by telling the audience 'I do not love to sit thus publikely' (I, ii, 198) as she sits *'in a Goldsmith's shop, at worke upon a lac'd Handkercher'* (I, ii, SD). Like both Jane Shore and Grissil, she is also signalling her suitability to act as the heroine of the play and be rewarded with the hand of the more sober gentleman while escaping the clutches of the wild young gallant.

However, Heywood gives the formula a more interesting twist by introducing another setting, more exotic than the others, in the house of the eponymous wise woman. The wise woman's house acts as the centre in which the plots are resolved and in which the dangerous and transgressive potentialities of the city comedy world are both offered and avoided. It is also the setting into which comes Chartley's abandoned betrothed, Second Luce, disguised as a boy. The Wise Woman displays her credentials as a white witch to a *'Countrey-man with an Urinall, two Women like Citizens wives,* Taber *a Serving man, and kitchin-mayd'* (II, i, SD). With this cast of gullible extras, the audience can share the superior position of Second Luce who comments on the trickery involved and, when she comes into the Wise Woman's service, has all the stratagems of prostitution, disposal of bastards and quack medicine explained to her.

Jean Howard has written persuasively of the ideological work done by the representation of a figure who so evidently transgresses official views of appropriate feminine behaviour.[2] However, the placing of the women characters in this comedy also has interesting implications for the representation and the construction of notions of popular culture. The Wise Woman has to *construct herself* for the audience, comparing her talents to

> Mother *Notingham,* who for her time, was pretty well skill'd in casting of Waters: and after her Mother *Bombye;* . . . Mother *Sturton* in *Goulden-lane,* is for Forespeaking: Mother *Phillips* of the *Banke-side* for the weakness of the backe: and then there's a very reverent Matron on *Clerkenwell-Green* good at many things. (II, i, 426–34)

This comic creation of an image of popular culture is, however, immediately identified with 'the Ignorant' by second Luce's observation

> What can this Witch, this Wizard, or old Trot,
> Doe by Inchantment, or by Magicke spell?
> (II, i, 442–3)

Her objection, interestingly enough, is not to witchcraft itself, or even the gullibility of the ignorant, but to popular appropriation of the prerogatives of learned men,

> Such as professe that Art should be deepe Schollers.
> What reading can this simple Woman have?
> 'Tis palpable grosse foolery.
>
> (II, i, 444–6)

Luce's opposition between deep scholarship and 'palpable gross foolery' sums up the artistic and ideological problem for the popular dramatist. The actions and settings for the play address their audience as 'realistic' in the presentation of urban locations and actual place names, and are distinguished from the arena of romantic comedy. However, they must also distance themselves from the low attractions of non-theatrical popular culture. In this play's case, 'palpable gross foolery' is restricted to the scene-setting; the plot, although it involves the Wise Woman's trickery, does not hinge on her magical skills so much as on the familiar conventions of new comedy both in disguise and in the set pieces such as the dialogue between the old men about their roaring days (II, ii,) or the sub-plot in which Sencer, disguised as a pedant, gains access to his beloved Gratiana and outwits the household tutor.

Heywood is able to adapt these comic conventions with further complications. Young Chartley, hoping secretly and falsely to marry Luce, is tricked into marrying his rejected, betrothed, Second Luce, disguised as a boy. This outcome would normally be used to end an action. Heywood, however, disrupts this neat closure by the chaos at the Wise Woman's house, giving scope for a further action in which Chartley goes on to pursue Gratiana and betray his friends. This permits a much more complex finale in which all of Chartley's victims are hidden around the stage to hear how he plots to use and abuse them. As each of his victims comes forward, he blames the plot on another one still hidden, and the simple, almost mechanical, plotting-device produces a crescendo of comic discomfiture.[3]

This reliance on plot for theatrical effect leaves little room for the complications of character and theme. Young Chartley, villain though he is, can be accommodated at the end by marriage to his original betrothed, second Luce, who, disguised as a boy, has engineered much of the plot in order to legitimate her marriage. When his plots falter, Chartley finds that the Wise Woman's tricks have 'lent me a glasse, in which I see all my imperfections, at which my conscience doth more blush inwardly than my face outwardly' (V, iii, 293–5). He is then rewarded by the discovery that the boy he had been tricked into marrying is a girl after all. Gallant behaviour is tolerated once it is recuperated into the acceptable forms of marriage and obedience to parents. The oppositions between rural and urban life, older and younger generations, high- and low-life are only in conflict for their potential permutations of plot. Like the city comedy of the boy players, the setting suggests a conflict of class: characters like Luce's father are simply described in class terms – 'Enter her Father, a plaine Citizen' (I, ii, 325 SD). However, that conflict has little theatrical dynamic and the resolutions, whose seeds are there in the original situation can be effected through marriage and reconciliation.

There are, however, moments when the play's realism, its authenticating representation of recognisable features of contemporary life, offer the possibilities of a more complex reading. A good deal of Young Chartley's dramatic vitality, for example, comes from the way in which he energetically repudiates the moral abstractions which are enforced at the end of the play. He replaces concepts such as honour, chastity and marriage with new commercial values. He mocks Boyster's earnest wooing of Luce with his own plot to seduce her and is clear how it will be achieved:

> in my pockett I have layd up a Stocke for her, 'tis put to use alreadie. And if I meete not with a Dyce-house, or an Ordinary by the way, no question but I may increase it to a summe. Well, Ile unto the Exchange to buy her some prettie Noveltie. That done, Ile visite my little Rascall, and sollicite instantly.
>
> (I, ii, 189–92)

A woman, for Chartley, is another commodity, like food or dice-play. However, his easy attractiveness to all the woman suggests some tensions between the play's stated and enacted morality, and a celebration of the potentialities of the new

London. It is impossible to associate consumption simply with the immoral figures. When Gratiana is brought to the Wise Woman's house for the play's denouement, she is persuaded by the possibility of a bargain of:

> an admirable suite
> Of costly needle worke, which if you please,
> You may by under-rate for halfe the valew
> It cost the making.

Getting and spending are not so central to the public theatre city comedies as they are to those of the boy players, but they tilt the action away from the simple morality and complicate the image of themselves offered to the public theatre audience.

It is significant that in *The Wise Woman of Hogsdon*, the active heroine, second Luce, is disguised as a boy. Her disguise releases comic potentialities in the plot where she is married off to Chartley but it also removes the character from both the domestic arena, where her action would be restricted to the roles of a wife, and the world of city comedy where her sexuality would be at issue.

For both Dekker and Heywood, the cross-dressed heroine offered a way out of the artistic and moral problems raised by the roles of women in domestic and city comedy. Cross-dressing released the heroine for a more active role in the plotting, making her the subject as much as the object of action. This was particularly the case in *The Roaring Girl* in which Dekker collaborated with Middleton to create a play centred on a real-life cross-dressing heroine. Unlike the heroines of domestic tragedy, Moll Frith was not presented as tied to the morality of marriage but as an individual who took a full part in the pleasures of London life. Arraigned before the Consistory Court of London, she confessed that

> she had long frequented all or most of the disorderly & licentious places in this Cittie as namely she hath usually in the habite of a man resorted to alehowses Tavernes Tobacco shops & also to play howses there to see plaies & pryses.

However, partaking of London's pleasures violated feminine

decorum and when she appeared 'at ye ffortune in mans apparell & in her boots & wth a sword by her syde' she drew attention
to that violation with the mocking challenge ' that she thought
many of them were of the opinion that she was a man, but if any
of them would come to her lodging they shoulde finde that she
is a woman'. Her challenge acknowledged the sexual nature of a
woman in such an unruly setting and yet Moll 'absolutely
denied' the sexual sin of 'beyng dishonest of her body' or acting
as a bawd to other women. She seemed to insist on the ability of
a woman to be unruly without being a prostitute, confessing
only to the general misdemeanours 'that she hath for this longe
time past usually blasphemed and dishonoured the name of God
by swearing and cursing & by tearing God out of his kingdom'
along with other 'Ruffinly swaggering & lewd company . . . cut
purses blasphemous drunkards & others of bad note.'[4]

Moll's offences could not be seen as sexual misdemeanours;
she had not borne a bastard or committed bigamy or failed to
fulfil a marriage contract. Her challenge to the social order was
no more than a challenge to its peace and good conduct.[5] She
gave 'her earnest promise to carry & behave her selfe ever from
henceforwarde honestly soberly and womanly' and the Bishop
was willing to 'further examine the truth of the misdemeanours
inforced against her wthout laying as yet any further censure
upon her'.[6]

The difference between Moll Frith and the other real-life
women of Elizabethan drama, Jane Shore, Alice Arden or Anne
Saunders, is important, for it determined the kind of play in
which she could appear. Her most obvious literary antecedents
were such legendary heroines as Long Meg of Westminster,[7] and
by basing the story of the play on the real-life character who had
worn men's clothes, Dekker and Middleton could capitalise on
fashion, give a truth to the popular theatre emphasis on real life
and at the same time play with the theatrical convention of
cross-dressing.

Dramatic convention provided clear roles and functions for
the cross-dressed heroine. The main plot uses an old-fashioned
version, in which Mary Fitzallard dresses as a man in order to
thwart the designs of the older generation and meet her lover
Sebastian. Moll's dressing as a man, by contrast, deceives no one
and seems much more threatening to old Wengrave who is

willing to allow Sebastian to marry Mary Fitzallard rather than make the much less suitable match in the masculine Moll. The two cross-dressed heroines exemplify the contrast made in Heywood's *Apology for Actors* between cross-dressing 'to beguile the eyes of the world in confounding the shapes of either sex', and cross-dressing which was held firmly in place by narrative convention 'to represent such a Lady at such a time appointed'.[8]

Dekker and Middleton use the theatrical potential of cross dressing to the full. Moll appears in the play both in and out of disguise. In the scene with the tailor (I, ii, 68–94), the awareness that she is a women gives a point to the jokes about a stiff yard or the width of her breeches, but in the scene with Laxton (III, i), cross-dressing provides a new twist to the normal disguise convention. Moll appears in disguise for her assignation with Laxton and when he fails to recognise her, she presses home the point of her identity. When he does eventually recognise her, the witty confusing of the sexes is compounded by the fact that he refuses to fight in unmanly fashion[9] and she insists on beating him to reinforce the lesson that indecorous behaviour is not the same as immorality.

Dekker and Middleton make clear the fact that they are extending the connections between dramatic fiction and the life-world of Elizabethan London. The prologue acknowledges that each playgoer

> comes
> And brings a play in's head with him: up he summes,
> What he would of a Roaring Girl had writ;
> If that he findes not here, he mewes at it.
>
> (Prologue 3–6)

Taste and fashion determine the form that the play will take, as much as the truth of Moll's life, and the Prologue goes on to contrast their Moll with other dramatic stereotypes, some of which Dekker and Middleton had used in their earlier collaborations. They do affirm that the play 'shall fill with laughter our vast Theater' (Prologue 10) but laughter will now come from life itself: 'She's cal'd madde Moll; her life, our acts proclaim' (Prologue 30). However, the laughter involving Moll Frith goes

further, offering to the public theatres new dramatic possibilities
for the connection between women and comedy. In the Prologue
Moll is distinguished from mere female equivalents of 'roaring
boys'[10] who offer no more than comic set pieces 'That beates the
watch and Constables controuls.' They also show that they will
not follow the conventional story of the 'Citty-Roaring Girl' who
outwits her husband 'And leaues him roaring through an yron
grate' (Prologue 17, 24). Moll's role in the play liberates her from
these conventional sexual patterns and allows her to act like the
witty swaggering gallants of city comedy who provide laughter
and dramatic energy. She initiates comic scenes like the set piece
of canting when Trapdoor and Tearcat come back to town and
are exposed by Moll's knowledge of low-life or the scene where
Jack Dapper is rescued from the sergeant set upon him by his
usuring father. However, it is difficult to build these set pieces
into an action for there are no models for a cross-dressed heroine
who neither seeks love nor betrays it. Like Julia in *Patient Grissil*,
the single woman can only lead apes in hell, for the conventions
of comic narrative demand closure in marriage. Each episode,
the gulling of Goshawke, the betrayal of Laxton, is set up and
resolved within a scene or two. Each of the scenes exemplifies an
aspect of London life. Sometimes, like the tiny vignette of the
tradesmen setting off with their water spaniels to hunt ducks in
Hoxton (II, i, 365–80), they celebrate the texture of citizen's
pleasures; on other occasions, and especially in the scenes with
Moll, they present a wit which has more to do with being
streetwise than with deceiving others. The action is loosely held
together with the new comedy action of Sebastian outwitting his
wealthy father and Wengrave's plot against Moll; but the main
dramatic energy of the play breaks with paradigms which
oppose men to women or citizens to gallants. When in Act V, ii,
the lovers reappear, married and forgiven, there is no surprise
and it is as if their framing plot carries the story which cannot
be Moll's. The process of their plot has not been fully dramatised
but by this stage it does not have to be. It can be taken as read
while the more interesting action takes place to one side of it but
cannot create a story for itself.

Nevertheless, the play, in engaging with citizen life and with
a notorious popular figure, cannot completely avoid the moral
implications of its action. Many commentators have pointed

out[11] that *The Roaring Girl* can be connected to the *Hic Mulier* controversy in which sexual identification is fundamentally linked to the good order of society. That controversy teased out the relationship between socially acceptable behaviour and sexual stereotypes in its suggestion that insubordinate women are a reaction to the foppishness of men, but it indicated how difficult it was to release the representation of women from the arenas of morality and sexuality. In the citizen wives plots, women's sexual fidelity is once again in question, even if the cliché of gallants seducing citizen women is overturned by the citizen women, like the women of *Westward Ho*, ultimately remaining chaste.

Testing a woman's virtue remains at the centre of the comic action (III, ii) as the uxorious Master Gallipot is gulled into providing thirty pounds for his wife to give to Laxton. Mrs Gallipot pretends that she was precontracted to Laxton and must buy off his claim. Master Gallipot, for his part, suggests the counter-claim that she is pregnant – the most important way of establishing the legitimacy of marriage – but when that does not work, is perfectly prepared to impugn her fidelity rather than lose ready money. The moral connections between marriage, fidelity and ready cash are comically overturned as Mrs Gallipot pushes him to understand that only cash will do as Master Gallipot is quite content to lose his reputation for the sake of thirty pounds.

For all their wit, Dekker's citizen women are honest, not because of conventional morality but because the gallants are such fools and are remorselessly anatomised as such:

> Because Goshawke goes in a shagg-ruffe band, with a face sticking up in't, which showes like an agget set in a crampe ring, he thinkes I'me in loue with him. . . . 'las what are your whisking gallants to our husbands, weigh 'em rightly man for man . . . (IV, ii, 16–72)

So powerful, however, is the connection between women and sexual narratives that Moll herself cannot escape the gallant Laxton's assumption that her free behaviour must denote sexual freedom. He is disabused and beaten, but Moll, like her real-life counterpart, had to insist on the distinction

> Cause youl'e say
> I'me given to sport, I'me often mery, iest,
> Had mirth no kindred in the world but lust?
>   (III, i, 99–101)

The question of the relationship between mirth and lust has enormous resonances. It denotes the possibility of separating social from sexual pleasure, of allowing women the same freedom to partake of the witty pleasures of the town without the imputation of licentiousness. However, it was a question which applied to theatrical fashion as well as to the real-life world of the audience. The resourceful young women of Shakespearian comedy who had cross-dressed in order to solve the plot had been replaced by the courtesans and gallants of boy player comedy whose wit was entirely directed at finding sexual rather than marriage partners. In *The Roaring Girl*, Dekker and Middleton opened up the possibility of a comedy which could go beyond the narratives of sexual exchange. However, for such a comedy action to be possible for women, they had to cross-dress in order to overcome theatrical as much as social convention.

The possibility of a new role for a woman character was also part of the experiment of Heywood's *The Fair Maid of the West*.[12] Its heroine, Bess Bridges, remains true to her lover Spencer and the play takes her through a number of adventures, including fighting with the Spaniards and a sojourn at the Moorish court of Mullisheg, before the two are miraculously reunited. Since Bess and her lover are separated from the beginning of the action, their love is never tested in social terms and can be used as the absolute of virtue, establishing Bess's credentials as a woman. Bess is therefore given a kind of social freedom to run her tavern and deal with ruffians without becoming involved in a sexual narrative. Certainly, all the comments about Bess raise questions about women's freedom. All through the play the villains question whether an honest woman can be so open and independent, but this question is not explored dramatically. Bess reassures the audience with soliloquy that she misses Spencer (II, i, 146) but in most of the action, her part could equally easily be taken by a man. Her competent management of the tavern at Foy is indicated by her dealing with questions over prices and keeping control over rough behaviour in her house, and these scenes are given variety by the comic exchanges with Clem, the clown, and the extended central episode with Roughman.

The Roughman sequence, like the Laxton sequence in *The Roaring Girl*, is constructed according to the classic *commedia dell'arte* scenario of the braggart soldier forced into a display of cowardice. Roughman boasts of his prowess as a fighter, beats the servants in Bess's tavern and insults the heroine. He then encounters Bess disguised as a page and she exposes his fundamental cowardice by forcing him to tie her shoes, untruss her points and submit to being straddled while she takes away his sword. In the *commedia* versions of this scenario the antagonists are usually men, but Heywood, like Shakespeare in *Twelfth Night*, used his heroine to vary the scene and increase the comedy. Bess and Clem joke about Bess's disguise as a man and she explicitly claims her ancestry in the legendary virago heroines:

> Methinks I could be valiant on the sudden
> And meet a man i'th' field.
> I could do all I have heard discours'd
> Of Mary Ambree or Westminster's Long Meg.
> (II, iii, 10–13)

The full comic potential of the scene is extended to Roughman's exposure. He assumes that his humiliation can be kept secret and returns to swagger in the tavern. He describes the terrible fight which he has passed through, and Bess allows him to wax eloquent on the theme before confronting him with the suit in which she has been disguised.

Her role as a virago is, however, given no more dramatic time, for the plot moves swiftly on to the scenes where Goodlack returns with the news of Spencer's death. He is anxious to prove that Bess has not remained true to Spencer in order to make off with her inheritance. However, the moving sorrow of her response to the news and her passionate farewell to Spencer's picture convince not only Goodlack that she is true, but also reminds the audience of the chaste woman's heart which lies beneath her witty and competent exterior.

One of the principal strengths of this play is the tight plotting which cuts between Spencer's fate and Bess's adventures. None of the sequences is overplayed and the speeches, with the exception of Bess's mourning are kept short and tight. By Act IV, Bess has used her inheritance from Spencer to equip the ship with which she will fight in his name, and the final part of the action deals with her heroism in the sea battle, her fleeting encounter with Spencer whom she has thought dead, and their final meeting in Mullisheg's court.

Even in Mullisheg's court, Bess's virtue is enough to quell the Turk's lustful plan to add her to his international harem and instead, she acts as the gracious benefactor of the Christians who have fallen under his sway. Most of the comedy comes from Clem's astonished reaction to his fortune. The pleasures of popular comedy in the mockery of foppish affectation are given full rein in Clem's parody of courtly behaviour, quoting *The Spanish Tragedy*, patronising the French and Italian merchants and, in the most hilarious sequence, narrowly avoiding the honour of being turned into a eunuch. The sexual tension of cross-dressing or moorish lust is all held at the level of this popular bawdy because the frame story of Bess's enduring love and Spencer's brave loyalty avoid the questions of passion and desire which might undermine moral certainty.

II

The first part of *The Fair Maid of the West* was set in the Elizabethan age and there is a possibility that it may have been written before 1604. It was published in 1630 along with a second part which, to judge from the style, was written significantly later. The style of the second part shows the influence of Fletcherian tragicomedy which women and their chastity are the central focus of the action which turns on sexual exchange.

The opening scene of Part II indicates the changes. Tota, Mullisheg's queen, is plotting revenge against her rival, Bess. She characterises both Bess and herself in terms of such essentialised qualities as 'womanish ambition', 'height of blood' or innocence unpolluted. Sexual passion is at the centre of this characterisation as she claims that she cannot live without the sexual attention of her husband:

> I should doubt
> I were a perfect woman, but degenerate
> From mine own sex, if I should suffer this
> (I, i, 12–14)

She tries to suborn both Clem and Roughman to betray their mistress and, though both refuse, the shift from their characters in Part I is clear from the tone of the dialogue she has with them. Clem is still the witty clown but his wit now has a sexual turn, rehearsing the misogynist clichés of boy player comedy:

> You shall meet some of them sometimes as fresh as flowers in May and as fair as my mistress, and within the hour the same gentlewoman as black as yourself or any of your Morians . . . why they put on their masks. (I, i, 78–84)

Moreover, whereas the joke of his castration had provided the farcical comedy of the narrow escape in Part I, in Part II he is a eunuch and makes bawdy play on it (Part II, I, i, 91 and IV, v, 99–100). Mullisheg, for his part, regrets returning Bess to Spencer, and tempts Goodlack to deliver her to him. Bess has lost her active role, and is the sexual object of others' passions. Mullisheg's vision of the feast that he will provide for her wedding which he will consummate, places her along with the other accoutrements of decadent consumption:

> The jewels of her habit shall reflect
> To daze all eyes that shall behold her state.
> Our treasure shall, like to a torrent, rush
> Streams of rewards richer than Tagus' sands
> To make these English strangers swim in gold.
> In wild moriscos we will lead the bride,
> And when with full satieties of pleasures
> We are dull and satiate, at her radiant eyes
> Kindle fresh appetite, since they aspire
> T'exceed in brightness the high orbs of fire.
> (I, i, 383–92)

The change of scene signals a change in what women represent and the kind of narratives in which they have a part. The audience is now assumed to be familiar with different narrative possibilities though their pleasure is still from seeing the conventions worked out. Roughman and Goodlack tell one another of the Moors' plot and the neatly obvious solution of putting the lustful Moorish king and queen together, hovers amusingly on the edge of consciousness as they rack their brains for a way out of the dilemma:

> GOODLACK. Brain, let me waken thee. 'Sfoot, hast thou
>   No project? Dost thou partake my dulness?
> ROUGHMAN. The more I strive, the more I am entangled.
> GOODLACK. And I, too. Not yet?
> ROUGHMAN. Not yet, nor ever. (I, i, 443–6)

This struggle to find a solution which is obvious within the conventions of the play is comic in itself and provides opportunities for comic performance. It also allows a further scene in which the plot can be slowly divulged to Bess and Spencer with comic dismay and suspense.

The bed-trick can then generate a number of further scenes in which Heywood extends the suspense by creating a complication as Spencer, Bess and their friends escape from the sleeping city. Spencer, disaster-prone to the end, is wounded trying to escape, owes his life to a worthy Moor, is released to save Bess from suicide at the thought of his death, but returns to certain doom in order to fulfil his debt of honour. Honour, like chastity is the abstraction which keeps the action moving from one disastrous brink to another and is also the key to the interim resolution which takes place half-way through the play, when Bess and Spencer are once more reunited and set off back home with Mullisheg's blessing.

This action, however, only gets them to the end of Act III. A Chorus explains that the lovers are parted once again on the high seas and Bess has once more to submit to assaults on her virtue, first by Banditti and then by the Duke of Florence who saves her from the first attempted rape. Bess's reactions also show how far the conception of her character has been changed. Assaulted by Roughman in Part I, she threatens him with the constable and stoutly defends her servants. The setting for her chaste fidelity to Spencer is a fully-realised social world in which her well-being and reputation are as much at stake as her virginity. Her reaction to the Banditti in Part II suggests, by contrast, an essentialised chastity which has no social concomitants:

> What, rape intended?
> I had not thought there had been such a mischief
> Devis'd for wretched woman. Ravish me?
> 'Tis beyond shipwreck, poverty or death.
> It is a word invented first in hell
> And by the devils first spew'd upon earth.
>
> (IV, i, 40–5)

A similar separation from the social world is evident in the view of men's honour proposed in the play. Women's honour had become completely subsumed into chastity and men's honour tied them to other men. The demands of honour were always at odds with commitment to women. In Act II, Spencer has to return from his escape with Bess to honour his promise to Joffer. In Act V, the Duke of Florence offers him an even more tormented bargain which means that he may never consummate his love for Bess nor tell her of his reasons. He goes in to see Bess sleeping but cannot break his promise

> that I should never, never
> Lie with her, being my wife, nor kiss her, touch her
> Speak to her one familiar syllable.
> Can oaths bind thus? My honesty, faith and religion
> Are all engaged.
>
> (V, ii, 27–31)

The painful ensuing scene in which Spencer refuses to touch his distraught beloved reworks the situation from Fletcher's *Wife for a Month* and is typical of the tragicomic style in which high emotion is wrung out of a completely artificial situation.

Heywood cannot resist turning the scene to comedy. Bess swoons in distress at her lover's seeming cruelty. However, he cannot touch her because of his vow and so, in anguish, leaves her on the floor. She is revived by the Duke of Florence, delighted to hear her lament that he 'would not speak, nor look, nor touch your Bess' (V, ii, 68). However, this is only one moment of variety in a series of surprising turns as Bess then swears to be revenged on Spencer and seems to be planning his death.

The emotional life of this play is intense as emotion is all there is to play for. The social setting, the moral dilemmas can all be changed for the sake of variety and the frame of reference is restricted to the models of other plays. Bess's father who

> Sold hides in Somersetshire' and being trade-fall'n
> Sent her to service
>
> (Part I, I, ii, 18–19)

is forgotten and she is as likely to compare herself to Portia or Lucrece (III, iii, 132–3) or be compared in her revenge against Spencer to the furies or Medusa. The touches of local colour or the use of real persons and location which created the authenticity effects of the melodramas of the turn of the century had been refined out of the action. In its place, were the emotions aroused by honour and chastity which had come to stand for the principles of men and women. The narratives of sexual exchange and encounter which tested the conventional morality of the citizen drama were replaced with a witty play with abstracted sexual feelings.

There is little sign here of the staunch feminist advocacy which Louis B. Wright attributed to Heywood.[13] Dekker and Heywood gave their strongest roles to heroines whose freedom of action came from being disguised as men, but even they could only take centre-stage when they were involved in stories which would end in marriage. By the end of Dekker's and Heywood's careers, that possibility was also more restricted as women characters had once again provided a focus for male concerns with honour and sexual control. In that dramatic world, women's sexual relations were their only claims to dramatic attention.

III

Dekker and Heywood's adaptation of the cross-dressed heroine shows both their creative ability to develop dramatic convention and the extent to which narratives focused on women had become the staple of dramatic writing. The issue of the erring wife and the comic focus on marriage had developed into a more wide-ranging representation made possible by putting cross-dressed women characters into roles and situations in which they could stand in for men. The problem of finding a narrative which could deal with a woman outside her sexual roles and relationship remained, but a return to real-life stories, as in the case of domestic drama, opened up new possibilities.

These dramatic possibilities for women outside of a domestic or sexual role were provided by the stories of two witchcraft cases, *The Witch of Edmonton* in which Dekker collaborated with Ford and Rowley and *The Late Lancashire Witches* which Heywood wrote with Richard Brome. Both plays showed professional companies making dramatic capital of contemporary affairs, but the plays also demonstrate the playwrights' abilities to adapt familiar dramatic form so as to make the most of the theatrical potential of the stories.

The Witch of Edmonton was based on the story of Elizabeth Sawyer who was tried and condemned as a witch and executed at Tyburn only weeks before the play took to the stage. The effects of collaboration are evident in the way the action works in scenes and loose-ends of plot are left untied, but the witchcraft plot provides coherence, uniting the plot of bigamy and murder with the comic action of Cuddy Banks in a powerful representation of the disruptive pressure of witchcraft on a rural community. In the speech which opens Act II, Elizabeth Sawyer questions and at the same time dramatises the unjust power of community pressures which force her eagerly to accept the power of evil forces when they are offered to her. She asks:

> And why on me? Why should the envious world
> Throw all their scandalous malice upon me?
> Cause I am poor, deform'd and ignorant,
> And like a bow buckl'd and bent together
> By some more strong in mischiefs than myself?
> Must I for that be made a common sink
> For all the filth and rubbish of men's tongues
> To fall and run into? Some call me witch,

And being ignorant of myself, they go
About to teach me how to be one.

(II, i, 1–10)

This speech vividly realises Elizabeth Sawyer's position as the outsider in a community which firmly polices aberration and gives a kind of credibility to the otherwise ridiculous business with the diabolical black dog who seduces her into witchcraft. However, the powerful sense of dramatic individuality which it creates and which has attracted modern actresses to the role,[14] also builds on the development of the defiant heroine in Dekker's domestic drama and its modification in the figure of *The Honest Whore* or *The Roaring Girl*.

When the witch makes her pact with the devil in the form of a black dog, Dekker emphasises its diabolic nature with a device borrowed from *Dr Faustus*. The dog insists that the witch sign the pact in her blood. At the crucial moment, the blood refuses to flow and is only restored when she curses again. This connection between cursing and witchcraft had been emphasised by Henry Goodcole's account of the story which was Dekker's source, but is given theatrical life by the echo which works equally powerfully even when the context is changed from the intellectual world of the magus to the low-life rural scene.

In the other witch scenes, Dekker also reworks dramatic raw material developed in his satires and earlier representations of women. One of the principle accusations against the real Elizabeth Sawyer was that she had caused her neighbour Anne Ratcliffe to run mad and kill herself. In these scenes, we see Dekker's and his collaborators' appreciation, both of the dramatic potential of the episode and of the available material with which to give it life. The representation of Anne Ratcliffe's madness drew on the style used in the Bedlam scenes of *The Honest Whore, Part 1*, developed by Shakespeare for Ophelia's mad scene and used by Fletcher for the gaoler's daughter in *The Two Noble Kinsmen*. Like Ophelia, Ann Ratcliffe speaks 'nothing/ Yet the unshaped use of it doth move the hearers to collection'. Like Dekker and Middleton's madmen, her 'nothing' draws on the material Dekker used and reused in his satires:

ANNE. Hoyda! A pox of the devil's false hopper! All the

golden meal runs into the rich knave's purses, and the poor
have nothing but bran. Hey derry down! Are not you
Mother Sawyer?

MOTHER. No, I am a lawyer.

ANNE. Art thou? I prithee let me scratch thy face, for thy pen
has flay'd off a great many men's skins. You'll have brave
doings in the vacation, for knaves and fools are at variance
in every village. I'll sue Mother Sawyer, and her own sow
shall give evidence against her. (IV, i, 180–8)

The mad scene, once again, suggests both an individual mind in
distress and a collective awareness of the ills of the world.

The same double effect of individual psychology and a more
general satiric view is evident in the scene where the witch is
questioned by the justice. At first, he ridicules and condemns the
villagers' efforts to charge Elizabeth Sawyer's witchcraft with all
the inconsequential ills that beset them. However, her response
generalises dangerously from her particular situation to the
accusation of witchcraft in élite society:

> What are your painted things in prince's courts
> Upon whose eyelids lust sits blowing fires
> To burn men's souls in sensual hot desires,
> Upon whose naked paps a lecher's thought
> Acts sin in fouler shapes than can be wrought.
>
> (IV, i, 105–9)

The satiric commonplaces which do not refer directly to her
situation, can nevertheless be integrated into the sense of her
character and the play's emotional action. They suggest that the
arrogance which had given her such dramatic presence in earlier
scenes had become her downfall.

Just as the original production must have negotiated the
complexities of witch-belief in early modern London, the play's
success on the modern stage depends on the extent to which it
corroborates modern views of the history and psychology of
witchcraft. In the 1983 Royal Shakespeare Company production,
directed by Barry Kyle,[15] Miriam Karlin created a powerful sense
of the emotional isolation and need which forced her into the
role of witch. The abject poverty of the social outcast was

visualised in her hovel on stage and her snarling exchanges with
the complacent and aggressive Banks put all the sympathy on
her side. Her ragged clothes and halting walk emphasised the
animal qualities which made her alliance with the black dog
understandable in psychological terms rather than as a dreadful
and sinful violation of the natural order. Miles Anderson's dog
was virtuoso performance which presented no contradictions
between his animal and human character. He managed to be
both a real dog and a symbolic figure; both comic and sinister.
His physical actions – rolling, fawning, snarling – created a full
relationship with both Elizabeth Sawyer and Cuddy Banks
which gave their characters the depth provided by their sense of
emotional need. The modern conception of witchcraft as victimisation of an innocent and misunderstood old woman was thus
fully realised by a performance which invited empathy, as much
as historical analysis.

The performance was necessarily informed by the modern
view that a belief in witchcraft was the product of the social
relations of early modern culture. The carefully authenticated
details of the wedding scene and the settings and furniture
created a fully-realised image of an early modern community.
The witchcraft itself was felt to need further explanation and its
connection to subsistence crises was dramatised in an interpolated dumb show where villagers ruefully discard the rotten
produce from their turnip crop. The play's continuing success on
the modern stage depends upon the appeal of fully-realised
characters in an easily-analysed social world. The moral and
theological issues dealt with in the original, are transformed into
psychological problems and a sense of an easy sympathy with
the victims of obvious injustice. This facile sense of injustice is
also extended to the religious context of the action. At the end of
the play, when Elizabeth Sawyer and the bigamous murderer,
Frank Thorney, have been executed, there is a moving moment
where Susan's father, in spite of his grief at his daughter's death,
welcomes Winifred, Frank's first, secret, wife into his family. He
is quite clear that Sir Arthur, Winifred's first seducer, has come
off lightly and the blame for the tragic sequence lies with him.
However, the rural community's resilience to tragedy depends
on its acceptance of human weakness and its ability to recon-
stitute the family life which lies at its heart. In Kyle's production,

however, religious superstition, seen as the source of injustice, was more emphasised and the cast assembled to sing, ironically, a verse of a hymn:

> The rich man in his castle
> The poor man at his gate
> He made them high and lowly
> And ordered their estate.

This simple correlation between superstition and an unjust social order is a travesty of early modern culture, but a generalised sense of a dark past, in which individual happiness is sacrificed to community norms, was all that was required. What the production could not explain was that the modern commonplace valuation of individual happiness and a critique of the society which prevented it, was at the heart of the dramatic developments made possible by Dekker's and Heywood's plays.

In presenting the witchcraft material in this way, Dekker and his collaborators were themselves entering a current debate about witchcraft. The complexities of witch beliefs were undergoing considerable change in this period[16] and that change was in part reflected in a contest over élite and popular attitudes to witchcraft. The playwrights' source for the play was Henry Goodcole's account of catechising Elizabeth Sawyer when she was in Newgate prison. Predictably enough, his account emphasised the importance of mortal sin and the active role of the devil; however, he was interestingly at pains to distinguish his account from that of 'base and false Ballets which were sung at the time of our returning home from the witches execution'.[17] The play steered a middle course between the most outlandish and incredible stories and the sober manifestation of providential justice. In part, it did so because of the mixed style. The story of Elizabeth Sawyer stands between Ford's tragic account of bigamy and murder, and the comic nonsense of Cuddy Banks and the bewitched morris dancers, but that mixed style was also a reflection of a new stage in the development of the theatre. The play was performed by the Prince's company[18] both at court and at the newly established Cockpit theatre. The Cockpit theatre was an attempt by the entrepreneur Christopher Beeston to create a new closed-in theatre like ones which the boy actors had established as fashionable earlier in the century. Beeston managed to gain a certain standing for himself, in spite of using playwrights and performers who had formerly worked at the down-market Red Bull.[19] The distinction between the popular and the élite theatres, and the rivalry established between their audiences was breaking down under pressure from the market, a market which also demanded collaboration among playwrights and entrepreneurs in order to meet the demand for plays.

A similar relationship between the demands of popular form and the cultural politics of beliefs about witches and women, was also negotiated in Heywood's collaboration with Brome on *The Late Lancashire Witches*, produced for the King's Men in 1632. The play was once again based on a current case of witchcraft and was staged before the judgement on the unfortunate Lancashire witches had even been pronounced. The circumstances of its staging show that even the mighty King's Men were not above the theatrical market-place and the need to appeal to popular interest, petitioning the Revels Office to prevent other companies using this witchcraft material.[20] The prologue makes clear that the play was meeting a gap in the market:

> Corantoes failing and no foot post late
> Possessing us with news of forraine State,
> No accidents abroad worthy relation
> Arriving here, we are forc'd from our own Nation
> To ground the Scene that's now in agitation.
>
> (IV, p. 188)

Unlike *The Witch of Edmonton*, this play does not deal with the making of a witch. The material taken from the trial proceedings is turned into a series of theatrically exciting set pieces whose tone is comic rather than sinister and in which the witches are both the performers of the mischief and the audience for its effects on the people of the rural community.

A central scene depicts the wedding between two servants from the bewitched households in which the images of rural festivity are turned upside down. A spirit snatches the wedding cake and 'poures down bran' (IV, p. 205 SD); the plate of mutton is turned into horns and when the pie is opened birds fly out of it. The fiddlers, like those in the Edmonton morris, play out of tune, disrupting the wedding dance, and in a later scene the witches feast on the food prepared for the wedding. These scenes of magic and witchcraft are primarily opportunities for comic display. The real accused witch, Mary Spencer, had confessed to playing a game with her pail, making it run downhill before her when she went to fetch water. The episode is turned into a scene where Mall, one of the servants, makes her pail come to her, presumably with the aid of an off-stage rope. It is an entertaining and simple theatrical trick suggesting conjuring rather than heretical witchcraft.

In the play's main action, witchcraft touches on more serious social issues as it turns upside-down the ordered world of patriarchy and degree. The younger generation of the household take to ordering their parents about, and the servants, in turn, show them no respect. As the characters say, the rare disorder

> 'breeds pity, and in others wonder,
> So in the most part laughter
> (IV, p. 181)

The inversion of social roles produces comic turns such as the servants' broad-country speech or the young man's complaint that his father 'was at the Ale Club but tother day and spent a foure penny' (IV, p. 82). Heywood's collaborator Brome had written a 'world upside down' play, *The Antipodes*, which included a gadding grandmother, and it is tempting to imagine him recycling the same material in the new context

The case of Mistress Generous, accused as a witch, is, however, treated more seriously and in the story of her husband's desperate unbelief that she could be a witch, Heywood echoes the dramatic tones and styles of *A Woman Killed with Kindness*. Master Generous describes his wife as a paradigm of godly wifehood:

> Of an unquestioned carriage, well reputed
> Amongst her neighbours, reckon'd with the best
> And ore me most indulgent.
> (IV, p. 93)

Like Frankford's characterisation of Anne, the statement sets up certain narrative expectations, but the play's comic witchcraft leaves no space to develop either character or situation. Moreover the account of how she had flown through the air and the incredible business when he finds that a strange horse is his wife metamorphosed, undermines the episode's serious tone. There is a serious dislocation between the absurd events and the high tragic rhetoric with which he announces his dreadful suspicions. Moreover in the same scene, the failings of women are treated comically as Robin the servant consoles his master with the reminder that all women are beasts. It indicates the way that misogynist rhetoric was part of the dramatic tool-kit which Heywood had at his disposal and was equally available for comedy or tragedy.

The comic and popular potential of witchcraft, perhaps similar to the 'base ballets' written on *The Witch of Edmonton*, was also evident in the current of bawdy which runs through the play. One of the witches, Margaret Johnson, in a moving deposition,[21] confessed that she had succumbed to the devil's sexual advances. In the Brome and Heywood play, the episode loses all its psychological particularity and becomes the occasion for bawdy when Peg remembers her 'sweet coupling' to the raucous amusement of her companions. Bucolic sexuality is also comically presented in the episode with two servants whose marriage is interrupted by witchcraft. The husband is given a wedding present of a codpiece point which renders him impotent, and much comedy derives from his wife's dismay at the failure of her expectations. She takes to beating him and the couple are subjected to a skimmington[22] in which the traditional rituals of social control are exploited for theatrical display:

> *Enter (drum beating before) a Skimmington, and his wife on a horse; divers country rustics as they passe Par. puls Skimmington off the horse: and Law Skimmingtons wife: they beat em. Drum beats alar. horse comes away: the hoydens at first oppose the Gentlemen: who draw: the clownes vaile bonnet, make a ring Par and Skim fight.*
>
> (IV, p. 234 SD)

This is the stuff of popular drama both in its representation of actual popular festivity and in its vivid theatrical effects.

However, the surrounding action places the sequence, and complicates our sense of the relations between popular culture and its audience. Parnell and Lawrence, the two servants, are participants in a popular ritual of shaming and exposure, but for the audience on stage, this low-life action is simply another show. Doughty, the gentlemanly spokesman for moderation in the play, is amused by the show and concludes the action by paying the participants beer-money. His condescending distance from the social implications of the scene is paralleled by the real behaviour of country gentlemen towards popular culture.[23] Whatever the actual character of the Globe audience for this play, it was invited to see itself as urban and élite, entertained by, but not implicated in, the representation of the pressures of rural existence. Doughty's amused attitude to the passions involved in the marital conflicts of the low-life characters offers a paradigm of the relations between an urban theatre audience and plays involving women's issues. Both the domestic melodramas of adultery and repentance, or the social conflicts of rural witchcraft became dramatic events, offering a series of theatrical pleasures mediating their treatment of the pressing social issues of gender relations or the special connection between witchcraft and women.

This tension between theatrical pleasure, serious social concerns and the status of the audience, is reflected in a unique contemporary account of the play discovered by Herbert Berry in the Phelips papers.[24] A letter from Nathanial Tomkyns records how he visited the Globe on the third day of the three-day run of *The Late Lancashire Witches*. It provides an unusually detailed account of 'the slights and passages done or supposed to be done by these witches' and concludes with a critical assessment:

And though there be not in it (to my understanding) any poeticall Genius, or art, or language, or judgement to state or tenet of witches (which I expected) or application to vertue but full of ribaldrie and of things improbable and impossible . . . in regard it consisteth from the beginning to the ende of odd passages and fopperies to provoke laughter, and is mixed with divers songs and dances, it passeth for a merrie and excellent new play.[25]

Tomkyns expected serious matter and the aesthetic pleasure of poetry, art and language from his visit to the Globe, but is prepared to settle for alternative pleasures of laughter, music and dancing. His tastes were apparently shared by 'a greater apparance of fine folk gentmen and gentwoemen then I thought had bin in town in the vacation'.[26] The forms of popular culture and indeed its social pressures had become the material for dramatic entertainment whether the audience was low-life or élite.

7

The Final Years

I

Both *The Late Lancashire Witches* and *The Witch of Edmonton*
appeared in the later part of the dramatists' careers, after a break
during which Dekker was in prison for debt, and Heywood
extended his writing into compilations of classical stories, a
prose account of the reign of Elizabeth and other non-dramatic
material.[1] The configuration of the theatrical scene to which they
returned was rather different. The King's Men playing at both
the Globe and Blackfriars dominated the theatrical scene, but
were challenged by Beeston who had organised the former Red
Bull companies at the new Cockpit in Drury Lane. Work for
Beeston dominated both dramatists' later careers[2] and showed
the continual experiment and variety of dramatic form which
was a mark of their professional engagement with all the
opportunities of the contemporary stage.

It is important to emphasise this variety for as Martin Butler
has shown

> Far too simplified assumptions about the workings of Carol-
> ine politics and the dependence of the dramatists on royal
> favour have produced a picture of the Caroline stage as

invariably expressing, monolithically and uncritically, the point of view of the King and his court. The reality was much more complex and much more interesting.[3]

Butler, to be sure, attempts to co-opt both Dekker and Heywood to the oppositional side, finding in the anti-Spanish attitudes of their plays evidence of a political opposition to the court. However, in the politics of culture, the dramatists' seemed concerned to reconcile the demands of theatrical pleasure with those of political allegiance. Heywood's explicit comments about his Caroline plays address the question of new styles, in particular his efforts to adapt sometimes recalcitrant material to the fashionable form of Fletcherian tragicomedy, even though he occasionally laments the decline of the drama from 'high facinorious things . . . to puling lovers craftie bawds and cheats'.[4]

In the prefatory matter to *The English Traveller* and in the play itself, these tensions are especially evident. The preface to the reader of the printed text includes Heywood's famous assertion of his involvement in 220 plays in which he had 'at the least a maine finger'. Only a handful of those plays are extant or even traceable; the hyperbole is part of Heywood's effort to insist on his own professional prolixity as compared with playwrights, like Jonson and Shakespeare, who had been honoured with collected volumes. His printing of *The English Traveller* was, moreover, an attempt to get the credit for a play which, he claims, was pirated by the printers, those other exploiters of dramatic talent. In the Prologue, Heywood presents another of his dramatic manifestos which signal his ambivalent relationship to the popular theatre. He begins by appearing to apologise that he has abandoned the style of the popular stage:

> We use no Drum, nor Trumpet, nor Dumbe show
> No Combate, Marriage, not so much today
> As Song, Dance Masque, to bumbaste out a Play

but he ends by asserting that 'He onely tries if once bare Lines will beare it' and offers, 'Some Mirth, some Matter, and perhaps some Wit'.

Everywhere, the play bears the mark of his attempt to adapt

his dramatic raw materials to a tragicomedy of sex and intrigue. The main action is taken from a story in his own collection of stories about women, the *Guneikeon*, in which Young Geraldine, the eponymous English traveller, befriends an old gentleman who has married a younger woman who was his former friend. The first part of the play teases the audience with the familiar narrative possibility that the traveller will betray the old man's hospitality, like Wendoll in *A Woman Killed with Kindness*. However, the essence of the new tragicomic style is to offer unexpected twists to familiar situations and this plot development does not come about. The characters in the play seem still caught in the old clichés and the traveller is accused of just such an infidelity in order that his unfaithful friend, Dalaville, can himself have an affair with the woman.

The play offers a mirror image of *A Woman Killed with Kindness* in dramatising scenes which do not occur in the earlier play and adapting others which do. The attractiveness of the young stranger is made evident when the wife's sister flirtatiously asks him about the beauties of other nations. The process of falling from love to adultery, which is puzzlingly absent from *A Woman Killed with Kindness*, is presented in the second act when Young Geraldine and the Wife find themselves alone, reminisce about their former acquaintance and agree that if the wife should be widowed she will marry him. However, that plot-development is closed off when his friend Dalaville suggests to Young Geraldine's father that his son's reputation is in danger and Young Geraldine is forbidden to see his friends again. The danger to Young Geraldine's reputation is entirely hearsay and depends on Dalaville's rhetoric, but all of the action depends on a pattern of assertion and suspicion, based on a knowledge of dramatic narrative as much as real behaviour.

Dalaville's subsequent adultery with the wife is reported by her servant Bessie who meets Young Geraldine in the market, and the whole dramatic impact of the plot development is given dramatic life in his ensuing soliloquy of anxious speculation. There is nothing in the action, or in the scenes with the wife to endorse or to undermine his suspicion. Her fidelity or adultery is only the source of suspense which animates the ensuing plan to visit her house at night, in order to explain his absence to her husband.

After he has explained his situation to the husband, Young Geraldine is persuaded to stay the night, and in a scene which once again echoes *A Woman Killed with Kindness*, he discovers the adulterers in the wife's bedchamber. The scene in the bedchamber off-stage is enacted in Young Geraldine's soliloquy which begins by identifying the voices he can hear and then moves straight into a denunciation of their lust:

> Unchast, impious woman,
> False to all faith, and true conjugall loue.
>   (IV, p. 23)

Like Frankford, he plans to murder them but is relieved to find that he cannot, as he has left his sword in his chamber! He resolves to go travelling once more, but before he does so, finds a chance to denounce the wife to her face so that she dies of shame while Dalaville escapes.

The wife, who is given no other name in the play, is given no opportunity to speak for herself or enact her role in the exchange of friend and lover. She is entirely created by their language. In the scene where Young Geraldine is forbidden to see his friends again, his dignified defence of their friendship suggests the possibility of friendship between women and men which is untainted by lust. However, from then on, the wife is simply a pawn in the action. She exists as a threat to relations with men, either by tempting Young Geraldine to disobey his father's wishes or to come between him and his former friend.

In their opening confession of their feelings, Young Geraldine and the wife agree that he might eventually and in due course take her husband's place. The action of the play allows Young Geraldine to become her husband's heir without this dubious undertaking. Women can effectively be excluded from the 'Marriage of Loue' which the husband confirms with Young Geraldine. In true tragicomic form, women exist to give excitement to transactions between men, and their demise touches no one with pity. The husband ends the play by asserting that they

> like some Gallants
> That Bury thrifty Fathers, thinkt no sinne

To weare Blacks without, but other Thoughts within.

(IV, p. 62)

The husband's recommendation of the behaviour of (by implication) unthrifty gallants is in keeping with the desired tragicomic tone of the ending but is completely at odds with his previous character as a hospitable and generous gentleman of the old school. It signals an uncertainty of tone which is even more evident in the play's other action which concerns the escapades of the rakish Young Lionel. Young Lionel has taken advantage of his father's absence to lead a riotous life and the plot presents the comic manoeuvres undertaken by his witty servant to keep him safe from his returning father's wrath. The plot works on a familiar comic formula taken from Plautus's *Mostelleria*.[5] At the end, Young Lionel is duly exposed but all accept that his behaviour should be seen 'Rather as sports of Wit than injuries'.

The sub-plot opens, however, on a quarrel between the servants which returns to the satiric preoccupation with old-fashioned values of stewardship. Reignald, the fashionable rake's steward, is turning the old retainer, Robin, out of doors

> Because thou stink'st of garlike, is that breath
> Agreeing with our Pallace, where each Roome,
> Smells with Muske, Ciuit, and rich Amber-greece,
> Alloes, Cassia, Aromaticke-gummes,
> Perfumes, and Pouders, one whose very garments
> Scent of the fowlds and stables.

(IV, p. 15)

Robin responds with anger that

> all that masse of wealth
> Got by my Masters sweat and thrifty care,
> Hauocke in prodigall uses

denouncing the young man's riot that has

> his modest House
> Turn'd to a common Stewes? his Beds to pallats

> Of lusts and Prostitutions? his Buttrey hatch
> Now made more common than a Tavernes barre.
>
> (IV, p. 16)

The moral force is all on Robin's side but Reignald is successful in evicting him.

Reignald's values and those of his rakish master are never completely endorsed and the satiric presentations, though eloquently expressed, occur in set pieces which seem out of place in the comic action. Confusingly, Young Lionel himself expounds them in a soliloquy where he compares a young man to a well-ordered household, ruined and undermined by lust. At that point, Young Lionel is teasing and punishing his whore's mother who has urged her daughter to attempt to exploit the wealthy young heir. The language of moral authority is used once again to denounce a woman, but the attitudes which it suggests are not carried over into the judgements of the rest of the action.

These scenes offer a false start to the action in which Reignald acts as the Plautine witty servant who keeps his master out of trouble, and Robin, the faithful retainer, only reappears in the final reconciliation. The comedy depends on a series of ever-more complicated manoeuvres to keep his the old master from entering the house and discovering his son's misbehaviour, and it is reinforced by comic monologues from a clown describing the young gallant's feasting. The clown purports to be shocked, but the comic virtuosity of his monologues seems rather to celebrate the excesses of the rake and his friends. The values of the new drama in which rakishness is condoned as youthful wild oats and wit is more entertaining than morals, sit uneasily with the morality of the popular drama and creates the same uneasy combination of styles which undermines the coherence of the play's main action.

The sub-plot of *The English Traveller* echoes the values of the boy player city comedy, but Heywood achieves this by going directly to the Plautine source of new comedy. Plautus had earlier been used by him as the source of *The Captives or The Lost Recovered*, licensed by Henry Herbert on 3 September 1624, for the Cockpit company. The action is based on the plot of Plautus's *Rudens*, in which two young women escape from their brothel-keeper during a shipwreck, take refuge with the priestess of

Venus and discover their true identity and their family, with the help of a casket drawn from the sea. By turning the priestess of Venus into a worthy abbot, Heywood is able to integrate the Plautus plot with a fabliau story of two quarrelling friars.

The play's manuscript provides fascinating evidence of the process by which narrative was turned into drama, and its details shaped for the stage. Heywood followed Plautus's sequence of events, and much of the dialogue involves an extension and elaboration of the situation in which he uses the proverbs, set speeches and question-and-answer routines which were the staple of the dramatic traditions in which he worked. In the opening scene, for example, Raphael tells his friend Treadway he is in love. Before he can move the action on by saying with whom or in what circumstances, Treadway rehearses the proverbial opposition to women and Raphael questions the logic of generalising from single examples. The debate draws on the quarrel over women but the terms of that debate have become automatic counters with no real engagement either in the play-world or the social world of the audience. Later, the sub-plot does turn on a woman's chastity, but in that case, as with the opening scene, the ideas and social values which underpin the action can be taken as read. The pleasure of the play lies in the complexities of narrative and suspense, increased by the localised pleasures of these witty exchanges.

This process of elaborating the action in set speeches and dialogues is extended by the two clowns, servants to Raphael and to the honest Ashburne who saves and protects the girls. Their dialogue is inflated and extended by mechanical rhetorical elaboration of lists and puns, and alliterative abuse. Raphael sends his servant to look for the procurer Mildew and he replies:

> who the (ffrenshe monsieur) (mean you), (Italian) Neopolitane
> Seignor the man makarel
> and marchant off madens-ffleshe, that deales altogether in
> fflawed ware, and crackt comodityes.
> the bawdy broker I meanes, where a man for his
> dollars may have choyse off diseases, and som tymes
> the pox too Iff hee will leeve beehind him a good
> pawne for it.[6]

The style is familiar from many of Heywood's clowns. The elisions and deletions of the manuscript illustrate, in detail, the elasticity of this method of composition. Not only is Mildew changed from French to Italian to Neopolitan but subsequent comic byplay with a payment to the clown is cut in order to move to Treadway's more serious worries about Raphael choosing his beloved from a brothel. Again and again, the clown extends the simplest dramatic action with comically vulgar and insulting rhetoric. After the bargain with Mildew has been struck, Raphael calls him back to insist on secrecy and the clown reiterates the command with

> stay oh thou father of fornication, and marchant of nothing but miseries and mischief, wheel about thou duncart of diseases. sayle this way thou galleyfoist of galls and garbage, dost not hear my master. Stay. (192–5)[7]

These lines could be cut in performance, as the comic double-act description of Mildew by Raphael and the clown is cut half-way down in the manuscript,[8] if the scene flags, or was extended if the clown was feeling inventive.

Each scene could be presented in a long or short version; at the beginning of Act II, Ashburne and his servant Godfrey watch the shipwreck which will bring everyone together for the action. They exit to help the castaways and 'Enter Palestra, all wet as newly shipwrecked and escapt the fury of the sea' (650 SD).[9] She has a soliloquy lamenting this unjust 'reward of Innocence'. In the manuscript, her soliloquy is cut by 28 lines and the entrance of her maid brought forward. The maid is also given an introductory explanatory soliloquy and from opposite sides of the stage each laments the loss of the other. These lamentations are also cut down in order to move the scene on to their reunion and their musical appeal for help to the inhabitants of the monastery. Each scene of this kind is a comic *scenario*[10] drawing on the literary and technical devices at the disposal of the professional stage.

These long-lived comic traditions are even more evident in the sub-plot of the two friars. Heywood's dramatisation followed the detail and order of events used in the version of the story told by Masuccio di Salerno[11] in a collection of anti-clerical novelle.

However, the gag in which a friar hits a dead body and then fears that he himself has killed it had been used both as a free-standing interlude and in other literary and dramatic narratives.[12] Heywood's play uses the same hilarious detail in the action but also creates scenes which economically combine plot-information with localised comedy. When the friars are introduced, the abbot, while reprimanding their quarrelling, also indicates that the monastery's founder and his lovely wife live next door. However, the scene's comic energy comes from the efforts that both friars make to disguise their mutual hatred from the abbot while making it clear to one another and the audience. Friar John insists that the ugly grimaces Friar Richard complains of are 'a weakness from my childhood' (l. 373) while Friar Richard insists he is not shaking his fist but has a congenital cramp that 'makes me weare clutcht fingers and that passion now came upon mee' (ll. 384–7).

This introduction sets the comic tone for the rest of the action. When the lady receives Friar John's letter of assignation, she is as much amused as offended, and her husband's rage at the impudence is out of proportion to the seriousness of the events. However, his role in the plot is to murder the friar so that the comic exchange of bodies can take place. Once again, the action is taken over by a comic servant: Dennis carries off the friar's body and deposits it in the monastery privy where the encounter with the enraged and incontinent Friar Richard takes place. Richard, thinking he had killed Friar John, carries the body back over the wall to the founder's house where the grotesque business in which the dead body is placed on a horse and chased from the city is devised. This plot affords no end of comic business – climbing over the wall with the body, the scene in the privy, and the predictable hilarity when Dennis finds the body again and thinks he has seen a ghost. The physical action is charted in the manuscript including a stage direction for '*A Noyse within Trampling of Horses*' (2743 SD) and instructions to the stage-keeper to act as a guard for Friar Richard when he confesses in terror to the murder. It also provides a group-scene for the finale when Friar Richard, falsely accused is led to execution and is reprieved at the last minute by the founder's confession; the founder in turn is saved by his wife bearing the king's pardon.

In all this comedy, it seems that Friar John is dispensable. He has to be killed in order to move from the anti-clerical adultery plot to the gag of the murdered friar. However, that transition seems less under control than other parts of the plot and the reasons for this are, once again, to do with Heywood's handling of traditional material. The plot with the founder's wife combines the comedy structure of all overlooking scenes with the serious attention to adultery and women's potential for infidelity which Heywood had addressed in *A Woman Killed with Kindness*. The combination is not only in the narrative material but also in the style. Having asked his wife to write to the friar, Lord Averne, like Frankford, announces that he will ride out after dinner and not return. The plot expectation of discovery and, at the least, disgrace is established. However, when Friar John gets the letter, the sexual vanity of his response is observed by Dennis and Lord Averne in a scene reminiscent of the episode with Malvolio in *Twelfth Night*. The tone of the rest of the plot moves uneasily from the force of Lord Averne's rage to Dennis's mockery and his grotesque comment, after the friar has been strangled, that

> I dare now
> Lodge him a whole night by my sister's side
> He's now past strumpetting.
>
> (1814–16)

This uncertainty of tone in the thwarted adultery plot is also caused by the way that some of Lady Averne's speeches catch the sense of a lived social world, preventing the smooth functionality required for farce. When she receives the letter from Friar John, her reaction suggests a complexity of character not found elsewhere. She is uncertain 'whether to smyle or vex'; she tries to understand Friar John's behaviour but also eloquently expresses the danger for women

> when every fayre woord's censurd liberty
> And every kind looke meere licensiousnes
>
> (1276–7)

She calms her husband's violent plan to blow up the monastery, insisting on the injustice of killing all, for the error of one. Just before her assignation, she clearly reminds him

> All offences are not (payde) woorthy deathe,
> Felowny, murder, treason and such like
> Off that grosse nature maye bee capitall
> Not folly error trespasse.
>
> (1736–9)

Unlike the play's opening discussion about chastity, based on the clichés of the debate over women, Lady Averne reminds the audience of a context in which adultery has real social consequences, and the murder of a friar cannot be just another joke.

In the play's main plot, too, the smooth comic action, the automatic exchanges of jokes and double act is sometimes stalled by statements about the nature of justice, and reflections on the rights and roles of women. When Raphael bargains with Mildew for his mistress, Mildew complains that she cannot be won to the trade of prostitution:

> neather promises, rewards
> example, or Intreaty fayre fowll meanes:
> gaine present or the hope off future goodd
> can force from her a presence then much lesse
> a frendly prostitution
>
> (162–8)

Moreover, like Marina in the brothel scenes of *Pericles*,[13] Palestra's very presence hinders Mildew's trade:

> For she hathe gott a trick to steale, my whores
> And such as off them selves are Impudent,
> When shee but coms in presence shee makes blushe
> As if ashamed of what they late had doon
> Or are about to doo.
>
> (179–83)

Later in the play when Mildew attempts to recapture the women, they are passionately defended by Ashburne who denies his right of ownership, insisting

> none is bredd with us
> but such as are free borne. and christian Lawes
> do not allowe such to bee bought or sould,
> for any Bawde or pandar to hyre such
> to Comon prostitution.
>
> (1544–8)

Heywood also draws on his populist tradition in having the women rescued not only by Ashburne who will be important to later plot-development, but by a band of 'country fellows' whose entry led by Godfrey produces the exciting stage action of 'A tumult within and suddene noyse enter att one doore Godfrey with coontry fellowes for theire reskewe at the other Mildewe Sarlaboys Palestra, Scribonia' (1496–8).

With its varied action, its music and jokes and its clever integration of five different character groups, this play is one of Heywood's most accomplished comic creations. However, in the moments where it seems to touch on more serious social issues, it reveals the tension in Heywood's evolving dramatic style. His commitment to the popular tradition with its concern for women and its celebration of popular direct action sits uneasily with sophisticated wit about adultery and sexual peccadillo, prevalent both in the Italian novella which was its source and in the Fletcherian comedy developed in this period by the King's Men.

II

The English Traveller and *The Captives* show Heywood at his most deftly professional, bringing together classical sources, his own work and the new dramatic styles, to create scenes of comedy and pathos. These plays engage with popular politics in their treatment of women and social concerns and in the way they situate the plays within a politics of culture. By the 1630s, Heywood seems also to have been more directly involved with adapting the politics of culture to the politics of state. Smuts has shown how anti-Spanish policies at court, supported by a Puritan opposition, were located in the circle around Henrietta Maria, Charles's French queen.[14] Heywood's work with Queen

Henrietta's Men at Beeston's Cockpit theatre may have involved more than a merely professional relationship

The heart of political conflict lay in the reluctance of Charles, and James before him, to come to the aid of the deposed Palatine prince who had married James's daughter Elizabeth in 1613. In 1632, the Palatine prince visited the court, and Heywood was chosen to write a prologue and epilogue to one of the entertainments provided for him.[15] His verses make clear his understanding of the politics of the visit, turning on the conceit of a lost eagle's feather 'which to regaine/She almost would give Almaigne, Rome and Spain'. The epilogue too, insisted on England's role as a leader in protestant Europe insisting

> So may none issuing from King Iames his stemme
> But be thought fit to weare a Diadem.
>
> (IV, p. 355)

For the most part, however, Heywood's politics were built into his activity as a professional dramatist. In 1633, he revived *If You Not Know Me You Know Nobody*, his play about Queen Elizabeth which, in the new political context, was a cultural gesture which explicitly supported those for whom Elizabeth's reign was an exemplar of militant Protestantism and a contrast to the politics of Charles I. The revived version of the play included a comic sequence in which effete Spanish courtiers joke about the possibility of seducing the English women, and mock Elizabeth's presumption as a woman to oppose their Armada. The style of the bawdy is that of Fletcherian tragicomedy, but it also reflects the old antagonisms based as much on religious as on sexual oppositions.

The nostalgic longing for the glories of a past age were, thus, as much a political as a cultural gesture, and it is in this context that the revival of even the less explicitly political *Jew of Malta* has to be seen. The prologue for the court production offered a disingenuous apology for its old-fashioned nature and a plea for its acceptance in that distinguished company; but in the prologue for the Cockpit stage, Heywood is more emphatic in his celebration of the great days of the Elizabethan theatre, represented by Alleyn and by Marlowe himself. Heywood seems to have seen himself as building bridges between the opposed factions in his insistence on continuity and an appeal to a broad audience. The dedication of the 1631 edition of *The Fair Maid of the West* reminds Sir Thomas Hammon that the play 'hath not onely past the censure of the *Plebe* and the *Gentrie*, but of the Patricians and the *Praetextae*:as also of our royall Augustus and Livia' (II, pp. 334–5).

The politics of culture and the state came together in the notorious affair of the puritan polemicist, William Prynne, who published, in 1633, an enormous compilation of anti-theatrical material, *Histriomastix*.[16] Among the familiar denunciations of the stage, Prynne unfortunately included an untimely marginal reference to 'women actors notorious whores' which seemed too pointed a reference to Henrietta Maria's own performances at court. Prynne fell horribly foul of official rage and was pilloried and mutilated. As the author of *An Apology for Actors*, Heywood was personally attacked by Prynne.[17] In his dedication of *The English Traveller*, Heywood, perhaps in response to Prynne, once again asserted the antiquity of the stage, promising that

> if they have been vilified of late by any Separisticall humorist, (as in the now questioned *Histriomastix*) I hope by the next Terme (*Minerva assistente*) to give such satisfaction to the world, by vindicating many particulars in that worke maliciously exploded and condemned.   (IV, p. 2)

No explicit rejoinder to Prynne was written but later that year, Heywood was involved in one of his most ambitious and successful projects which, at least by implication, mocked Prynne's philistinism and reiterated some of Heywood's changing perceptions of the relationship between the theatre and the changing social relations of culture.

Love's Mistress, or The Queen's Masque is one of Heywood's most ambitious works and its relationship to the context of its production illustrates the complexities of Caroline cultural politics. The play was performed at the Cockpit theatre but was also chosen for production at Denmark House on the occasion of the king's birthday, and again for the queen's birthday in the same week. The court performance was made more splendid by the work of the court masque designer, Inigo Jones

> Who to every Act, nay almost to every Sceane, by his excellent

Inventions. gave such an extraordinary Luster; upon every occasion changing the stage, to the admiration of all the Spectators.

By 1634, Heywood had come under the patronage of the Earl of Dorset who, as Lord Chamberlain, would have been instrumental in arranging the court performance and in securing the services of Inigo Jones. This courtly patronage of a professional dramatist raises interesting questions about the relationship between professionalism, patronage and politics. David Bergeron has used this and other evidence of aristocratic patronage to suggest that Heywood was seeking to distance himself from his professional work. Heywood's biographer put it more strongly, asserting that 'Heywood now restored to self-respect and the dignity of an artist by the royal approval, had resolved no longer to live for the rabble.'[18] He suggested that *Love's Mistress* is to be seen as an allegory of the Prynne affair and describes the play as 'Heywood's real revenge', adding 'Such an adversary of humane letters Prynne appeared to his age to be, and we have no hesitation in equating him with Midas or in identifying the overgrown child of his brain with Midas's clownish bastard.' Neither the play nor Heywood's career endorses this view. The play was also performed at the Cockpit, and Heywood did not cease writing for the professional stage after his success at court. However, Dorset's patronage and the context of the Prynne scandal does offer an interesting complication in the way this play can be read. The play's most explicit connection with topical concerns is in its representation and discussion of platonic love. It is based on the story of Cupid and Psyche which deals with the distinction between true love and love based on sight of the beloved. Similar ideas informed the cult of platonic love, which was both a style of behaviour and a set of courtly principles which were associated with Henrietta Maria's circle. The cult became explicitly connected to Prynne's attack on the queen and to Heywood's play through Dorset. At Prynne's trial, Dorset defended the queen herself against Prynne's attack, describing her as an

Example to all Vertues . . . and as a Woman so constant for the redemption of all her Sex from all imputation, which Men (I know not how justly) sometimes lay on them.[19]

As Lord Chamberlain, Dorset could be expected to defend plays, but he extended the defence to questions of sexual politics which are then taken up in Heywood's play which he supported at court.

The play also offers a complicated defence and analysis of art. It addresses the question of the social worth of poetry and the problem of educating a popular audience in the appreciation of dramatic art. Apuleius, transformed into a man, seeks the muses' spring and encounters Midas who mocks his search for poetic beauty. In response, he shows him the story of Cupid and Psyche, and the rest of the action presents the story interspersed with a set of contests in which Apuleius offers Midas an image of the kind of entertainment favoured by him and his kind. In the first inserted contest, Midas rejects the scenes he has seen of Venus and Cupid, and Apuleius entertains him with an anti-masque of satiric shows representing the dancing figures of a proud, a prodigal, a drunken and an ignorant ass, together with the stock satiric figures of 'A young Gentlewoman' and a usurer. Apuleius also offers an allegorical explanation of the action with Cupid and Psyche, presenting it as an image of the soul's search for perfect love. In the second anti-masque, Midas chides the clowns for their subservience to Cupid and denounces Apuleius and his artistic efforts. He tells the country swains that Cupid is maintained only by poets whose folly is evident in the lies told by Homer. He offers a low-life version of the epic of Troy in which 'Troy was a Village of some twenty houses', Agamemnon 'the high Constable of the hundred', Ajax a butcher, and Hector a baker! (V, p. 113)

The comic energy of this parody and its connections with the domestication of the Troy story in Heywood's own *Iron Age*, suggest that Heywood's position on art and the populace is not a simple one. In a subsequent interlude, Midas presents Apuleius with a dance of 'Swaines and Country Wenches'. Apuleius's initial condescending view that 'Art sometimes must give way to Ignorance' is replaced with pleasure 'with your Pastoral mirth' while maintaining the distinction between the art which feasts the eyes and the higher form which requires 'attentive eares'.

Later in the play, the division between high and low art is made more explicitly and more angrily. The famous contest between Pan and Apollo is enacted on stage.[20] In spite of the appalling doggerel offered in praise of Pan, Midas and the clowns award him the prize and are passionately denounced by Apollo

> Henceforth be all your rurall musicke such,
> Made out of Tinkers, Pans and Kettle-drummes;
> And never henceforth may your fields bee grac'd
> With the sweet musick of Apollo's lyre.
>
> (V, p. 127)

Apuleius takes a more tolerantly condescending view of low taste in music. He acknowledges the need to 'suite me to thy low capacitie' but offers visual pleasure as well as noise:[21]

> Of Vulcan's Ciclopps Ile so much intreate,
> That thou shalt see them on their Anuile beate;
> Tis musicke fitting thee, for who but knowes,
> The vulgar are best pleas'd with noyse and showes?
>
> (V, p. 146)

Apuleius mitigates Apollo's uncompromising contempt for low taste. He recognises, as Heywood had in his city pageants and his Age plays, that visual, physical drama, such as might please an unlettered audience equally provided scope for invention, and indeed could draw effectively on the classical tradition.

The clown's philistinism is punished by being struck with Cupid's arrow. As a result, he aspires to the *furor poeticus* which might win him Amaryllis's love. Love, of course, creates only false poets whose sole subject is the beloved and her beauty. The clown's false poetry is familiar mockery of low poetic aspiration, but in this context it also tries to make a more complex distinction between the low and high motives for poetry, connecting them to true and false love. Heywood's distaste for the poetry of sexual conquest is evident, not only in the contrast between the clown's passion and that of Cupid, and also ties in with the pure ideals of platonic love espoused by the queen.

In the main action, Psyche fails in her love affair with Cupid when she agrees to her false sisters' advice to steal a look at him when he is sleeping. The looking with the eye and not being content with the mind is her downfall and results in her, and by analogy all women, being punished with perpetual unrequited passion. Her disobedience to Cupid, and Venus's angry spite, also transform her beauty into an image of an ugly diseased whore who is rejected by the father and sisters whose curiosity was her first downfall. She is also forced to perform a series of impossible tasks for Venus; with the help of Cupid and Mercury, she obtains the box of beauty from Proserpine but, inevitably, falls prey to the temptation to use it on herself with disastrous consequences. Psyche and the clown are then connected by having the clown steal the box and making himself uglier than ever. Eventually, Psyche is forgiven and restored to beauty by Jove's intervention and the play ends with a consolatory image of harmony in a dance by Cupid, Psyche, the gods and goddesses.

Harmony, it seems, can be restored by the godlike artist. However, it is constantly under threat not only from the lower orders but from the destructive passion of women. The connection between women and popular culture which had appeared in the mockery of domestic drama in the élite culture of the boy players reappears in Heywood's sense that the deformations of the new forms of Caroline theatre are equally infected by women. In this play and in *The English Traveller*, women are presented both as the passive victims of men's sexual conquest, but also as the inevitable sources of disruption and disharmony. At the allegorical level, Cupid's love for Psyche can represent the pure love for the platonic soul; but insofar as the soul is a woman she can only produce disruption and discord and must be reminded of the evils of her insatiable passion and its location in the diseased body of a whore.

Heywood's interest in the cult of platonic love may have had more particular implications than his intellectual concerns with high and low culture. The platonic theme and its discussion of true and false, physical and spiritual love, may have flattered the queen's interests in the cult of love which she had instigated at court. However, Apuleius's insistence on the importance of the allegorical meaning also shows the extent to which dramatic art was defended according to its capacity to embody moral truth.

The form of *Love's Mistress* made its own artistic statement. In combining the dances, shows and classical material with allegory, Heywood was taking the dramatic form which he had used in the Age plays a stage further.[22] The overall effect combined the pleasures and, indeed, the ideology of the court masque with those of the professional theatre Though it is clear that for Heywood, the art of shows was a lesser form than the direct access to truth offered in allegory, the play as a whole offered the reconciliation between the forms of high and low art. It may have equally reflected Heywood's aspiration for a unified artistic culture ensured by the patronage of the court itself.

III

Dekker's work for Beeston's companies at the Phoenix also demonstrates his efforts to adapt to the new styles of the later Jacobean and Caroline theatre. His first play after being released from prison was *Match Me in London*, licensed in 1623 for performance by the Lady Elizabeth's Men at the Phoenix.[23] Hoy describes the play as Dekker's 'gallant attempt to grapple with the new style in playmaking' though he also notes that 'Virtually every character type and every dramatic situation had its original in some earlier Elizabethan or Jacobean play.' The influence of Fletcher's tragicomedies is evident in the framing action in which the king repeatedly tries to seduce Tormiella. In a scene which directly echoes both *Valentinian* and Middleton's *Women Beware Women*, Tormiella is taken to court and separated from her servants and protectors. The king is told of Tormiella's arrival in the town by Dildoman, the procuress, a figure familiar from Fletcher's 'lustful tyrant' plays.[24] However, having accepted her temptations, the king, in a characteristically tragicomic reversal, refuses the offered seduction when Tormiella comes to court and instead denounces the bawd with all the rhetoric of moral rectitude.

These twists and reversals, the endless circling round a potentially disastrous situation, together with the sub-plot of an attempt to poison the king, present a superficial resemblance to the Fletcherian style. However, the motif of aristocratic seduction, and the contrast between a citizen woman and a corrupt court had been used before Fletcher. Indeed Dekker and Heywood in *Patient Grissil* and *Edward IV*, both written for the public theatres, had initiated the use of sexual confrontation as a dramatic narrative. The conflict between citizen and aristocratic values evident in those plays, also emerges in *Match Me in London* together with the key devices for its dramatic realisation. As in *Edward IV*, the king first encounters Tormiella in her shop and, like Hippolito in *The Honest Whore, Part 2*, his situation is domesticated in a coded discussion between himself and his queen which talks of the sun and his choice of flowers. As in *Edward IV*, the queen and concubine are brought together and the dramatic potential of their rivalry resolved in the recognition that their womanhood overcomes the conflict between them.

The politics of the play also reflect those of the popular rather than the élite audience. Dildoman's villainy is emphasised by her contempt for Tormiella's husband; 'A flatcap, pish, if he storme, give him a Court-Loafe; stop his mouth with a Monopoly' (I, iv, 139–40). And the women express their solidarity as contrasted with the commercial sharp practice:

> Since we must needs be sharers, use me kindly
> And play not the right Citizen, to undoe
> Your partner, who i'th' stocke has more than you.
> (III, iii, 55–7)

The emotional investment of low-life figures in their domestic happiness expressed by Matthew Shore is also emphasised in the scene, echoing *The Shoemaker's Holiday*, when Cordolente, Tormiella's husband, brings her a pair of shoes. He tries to carry it off with witty bawdy about drawing on shoes and making them fit but cannot sustain the game and breaks down.

Match Me in London indicates some of the difficulties of locating the professional dramatists in an opposition between élite and popular culture. The anti-Spanish attitudes which might be assumed from the play's setting in a corrupt Spanish court, are complicated by the king's integrity and his ultimate refusal to exercise his lustful power. Moreover, Dekker attempts to adapt essentially popular dramatic motifs to the styles of Italianate revenge and Fletcherian tragicomedy but the result is confused and the play is most dramatically successful when handling domestic situations or in the passionate opposition of

Tormiella's father to the king's efforts to buy him off with courtly favour. However, this apparent commitment to the values of the public theatre is somewhat compromised by Dekker's dedication of the 1631 edition of the play to the courtier dramatist Lodowick Carlell. In a blatant request for courtly patronage, he writes 'Glad will you make mee, if by your Meanes, the King of Spaine speakes our Language in the Court of England' (Dedication, ll. 11–12). The play offers a much stronger sense of the professional dramatist, taking the opportunities offered by a changing theatrical environment and using his dramatic stock in a new market.

A similar theatrical opportunism combined with complex and contradictory political material is evident in Dekker's collaboration with Ford in *The Sun's Darling*. This combination of allegory and shows, offered a curious hybrid of spectacle and narration, described by Henry Herbert in his licence for the Phoenix as being 'in the nature of a masque'. The play is structured round a journey as Raybright travels to the courts of each of the seasons. He encounters Humour and Folly who accompany him on his journey, and, like medieval Vice figures, tempt him away from the virtues of each court. At the end, Raybright reaches the court of Winter and is tempted to follow Humour through the whole cycle again but is intercepted by the Sun himself who reminds him

> Thy sands are numbred, and thy glasse of frailtie
> Here runs out to the last: here in this mirror
> Let man behold the circuit of his fortunes.
>
> (V, i, 304–6)

The Sun's account of the allegory's meaning in the final speech has the elegant coherence of the familiar correspondence between a man's life and the seasons. However, the allegory provides only the barest scaffolding on which to hang a variety of shows, dances and satirical set pieces. Each of the seasons' courts is characterised by a dance. The Spring, accompanied by Health and Delight offers a morris of 'Rurals' dressed in 'country gray'; Summer shows a dance of haymakers, and Autumn, accompanied by Cupid and Fortune, offers both honour and the bounties of the earth. On every occasion, Raybright scorns their gifts, preferring to move on to the next court with Humour and Folly.

Each of these encounters with the seasons makes both a political and an artistic statement. Spring tells Raybright that rural folk 'seldom ploughs treason' and fears that Raybright will be stolen away by great ones. This contest between simple country delights and more sophisticated pleasures is presented by an opposing dance of 'a Souldier, a Spaniard, an Italian Dancer, a French Tailor' and in the ensuing argument, Raybright chooses between the delights of Health and Youth and the commodities offered by Humour and Folly. Throughout the play, the allegory depends upon a contrast between the pleasures offered by the seasons and the mockery and vain variety with which Humour and Folly tempt the hero. The structure is similar to the morality play but where the medieval drama could make a clear distinction between virtue and vice, this more secular play can only contrast true love and honour with the comic mockery afforded by Raybright's flighty companions. In the court of Autumn, Fortune and Cupid speak of the whole range of pleasures that they can offer Raybright. Some of them, like 'bright honour' or being a warrior fit very easily into existing moral paradigms, but Fortune and Cupid also offer the possibility that Chastity will be rendered servile, and suggest that Raybright should become a merchant which seem more puzzlingly related to the moral or political oppositions being drawn up. Moreover, faced with this list of abstractions, Folly and Humour are simply rude, making jokes about the flatulent nature of Autumn's gifts and offer a drunken song and dance in honour of wine. The demands of theatrical variety and local poetic pleasures swamp the meaning at every turn.

The politics of the play, are much more explicit in the final sequence which takes place at the court of Winter. The scene opens with a comic exchange among some clowns who fear that the expected arrival of Raybright will bring them nothing but cuckoldry. These clowns are the opposite of the Rurals in country gray who welcomes Raybright to the court of Spring. They are severely reprimanded by Winter for daring to plot to oppose 'Your Prince's entry into this his land' (V, i, 22). Their rebellion is more explicitly connected to current religious controversy by the suggestion that the new prince 'would bring new laws upon us, new rights into the Temples of our gods' (V, i, 49–50). However, that explicit political concern does not build on anything in the rest of the play, and indeed offers a view of Raybright which is quite at odds with the vain and idle companion of Humour and Folly who has danced through the previous scenes.

This curious change in tone and style in the final act of *The Sun's Darling* points to a change in the original design of the morality action, and has caused critical debate over the dating and implications of the evident additions to the text. Bentley has argued that this scene with the peasants was interpolated into the text in 1638/9 and refers to the Bishops' wars, when a force was sent to subdue the Scots, rebellious over the imposition of religious change. Jerzy Limon, on the other hand, argues that the additions were made closer to the time of the first performance at the Cockpit in 1623. He suggests that the original play was planned for the return of Prince Charles from his Spanish adventure and that its text was

> re-written and adapted for a public stage, with the intention of evoking in spectators particular associations with the political situation of the day, and through these associations to draw attention to England's obligation to enter the war for the recovery of the Palatinate and Bohemia.[25]

For Limon, Raybright is Charles, son to James I, and his dalliance in the various courts is an allegory of his disastrous courtship of the Spanish Infanta. His final triumph in Winter's court is a wishful fantasy of his hoped-for role as the defender of Palatine interests in Europe. Winter's bride, Bounty, to whom Raybright swears allegiance is Charles's sister Elizabeth, often called the Winter Queen and the 'queen of hearts'.

There is, however, only a partial fit between this allegorical reading and the text. Raybright's death at the end of the scene does not fit the fantasy of Protestant glory and to connect his weak and vacillating character to the heir to the throne would be dangerous indeed. The clown's anxiety about the changes to religion and the clear reference to the action taking place in the north, gives some support to Bentley's reading. However, it is at odds with Dekker's Protestant sympathies which were so evident in *The Whore of Babylon* and so begs the question of the author of the interpolations. Topical readings inevitably leave gaps and inconsistencies because of uncertain knowledge of all the historical details of texts, authors and particular circumstances. However, these possible readings of *The Sun's Darling,* together with the satire which informs all the dramatic contests which make up the action, do indicate the continued engagement of the theatre with the pressing political questions of the time.

Throughout Dekker's and Heywood's careers, the interconnected politics of culture, class and faction provided the live wires which connected their drama to their audience. However, their plays were also created in a context provided by the material circumstances of a developing professional theatre and deployed the forms and conventions available to theatre-writers at the time. Both dramatists were innovators, adapting history and domestic narratives of love and sexual conflict to fill the stages and attract an expanding audience. Few of their plays have survived into the classic repertory of the modern theatre but in understanding the pressures and possibilities of their professional drama we are better placed to understand the complex determinants of early modern culture as a whole.

8
Conclusions

In the programme notes to the 1986 production of *The Fair Maid of the West*, Trevor Nunn described Heywood as 'an entirely accessible, popular entertainer whose achievements provide a fascinating context for his greater but more obscure contemporaries'. For that production *The Fair Maid of the West* was rewritten to combine the two parts into a manageable single production and to give a stronger focus to the central figures. It was presented with extraordinary physical gusto, using all the levels and the whole of the Swan auditorium for its exciting chases and sea battles in which the actors swung on ropes over the heads of the delighted audience. The 1991 RSC production of *A Woman Killed with Kindness* tried to provide a religious motif to explain the motivations of the action. They did so through a curious combination of pagan and Catholic religion which involved genuflection before a Celtic cross and the use of corn dollies and other signifiers of rural superstition. The energetic young fringe group that produced *The Honest Whore* in 1992 in the auditorium of Raymond's Revue Bar, a famous strip-club in London's Soho, dressed the play in the 1950s, a period vaguely representative for youngsters in the 1990s of past repression. The whore was a night-club singer and the opening funeral processed through the auditorium accompanied by music from a live jazz band.

All of these productions, and that of *The Witch of Edmonton*
discussed in Chapter 6, indicate something of the way in which
Dekker's and Heywood's plays are seen and produced on the
modern stage. Directors and audiences recognise the emotional
power of the situations they dramatise, but are also aware of the
way that the characters are embroiled in problems that arise as
much from their historical circumstances as from their particular
psychology.

Given these interests and presuppositions, modern directors
seem most attracted to Heywood's and Dekker's domestic
melodramas and plays, which offer a fairly recognisable image
of the early modern period. What is left out is the enormous
range of their work in political drama, the theatrical experiment
with visually exciting shows tied to allegory and the celebration
of popular mythology in their citizen drama. These plays are tied
to their historical circumstances in a rather different way. They
provide a way into understanding the relationship between
plays and the cultural moment into which they are produced and
the way in which the drama itself constructed the categories of
popular theatre.

The popular theatre was not simply a matter of buildings,
seat-prices and audience into which the drama was placed. It
was a matter for negotiation among theatrical traditions, kinds
of narrative, the tension between visual and verbal dramatic
form, and political ideas, as well as the material conditions in
which they were enacted. This book has shown how narratives
of women, or rebellion, of history and of the mythology of
citizenship were the key counters in this negotiation. They were
intermittently connected to topical political issues of state and
religion and foreign policy but they were also embedded in a
wider politics of gender and social conflict through the use of
satire.

Dekker and Heywood were important figures in this negotiation of a politics of culture because they debated the issues
explicitly and because they were active over such a long period
of social and political change. As professionals, they were often
forced by the pressures of events and commerce to use their
theatrical toolkit in a variety of expected and unexpected ways.
As such, an understanding of their work can modify the simple
oppositions that emerge from some attempts to make the politics

of early modern culture into a costume drama version of our own. But, perhaps more importantly, an awareness of their constant experiment with dramatic form and the sheer variety of their work help an appreciation of drama which provides familiar as well as new theatrical pleasures, which is self-reflexive and which alienates, as well as engages its audience. Not all of that drama would satisfy the taste of audiences in search of a kind of prose Shakespeare, but they can surely find a place in the eclectic theatricality of the modern stage.

Notes

1 Fireworks All Over the House

1. See the preface to John Webster, *The White Devil*, ed. John Russell Brown (London: Methuen, 1960).

2. On the continuing and changing reputation of Shakespeare, see Gary Taylor, *Reinventing Shakespeare, A Cultural History from the Restoration to the Present* (London: Chatto, 1990).

3. See Kathleen McLuskie, 'The Poets Royal Exchange: Patronage and Commerce in Early Modern Drama', *Yearbook of English Studies*, vol. 21 (1991) 53–62

4. See Roslyn Knutson, 'Henslowe's Diary and the Economics of Play Revision for Revival 1592–1603', *Theatre Research International*, vol. 10 (1985) 1–18; G. E. Bentley, *The Profession of Dramatist in Shakespeare's Time, 1590–1642* (Princeton, NJ: Princeton University Press, 1971); Neil Carson, *A Companion to Henslowe's Diary* (Cambridge: Cambridge University Press, 1988). See below pp. 145–54 for Dekker's involvement in dramatising the story of the Witch of Edmonton, and Heywood's in dramatising a case of Lancashire witchcraft.

5. This has led some critics to overemphasise the importance of patronage at the expense of commerce. See D. Bergeron, 'The Patronage of Dramatists: The Case of Thomas Heywood', *ELR*, vol. 18 (1988) 294–305.

6. *Henslowe's Diary*, ed. R. A. Foakes and F. T. Rickert (Cambridge: Cambridge University Press, 1961) p. 23. Discussed in A. M. Clark, *Thomas Heywood, Playwright and Miscellanist* (New York: Russell & Russell, 1958) pp. 10, 11 (hereafter referred to as *Thomas Heywood*) and Carson, *A Companion to Henslowe's Diary*, p. 60

7. While working for companies financed by Henslowe, Dekker worked with Chettle, Haughton, Day and Drayton.

8. Cyrus Hoy, *Introduction, Notes and Commentaries to Texts* in *The*

Dramatic Works of Thomas Dekker, 4 vols (Cambridge: Cambridge University Press, 1980) vol. III, pp. 139–42.

9. Dekker collaborated with Webster on *Westward Ho* and *Northward Ho* (see below pp. 107–15); with Middleton on *The Honest Whore, Part 1* and *The Roaring Girl* (see pp. 115–27, 133–8); with Ford on *The Witch of Edmonton; The late Murder of the Son upon the Mother* and *The Sun's Darling* (see pp. 145–50, 175–8).

10. Andrew Gurr, *Playgoing in Shakespeare's London* (Cambridge: Cambridge University Press, 1987).

11. Dekker, *The Wonderful Year*, in F. P. Wilson (ed.), *The Plague Pamphlets of Thomas Dekker* (Oxford: Clarendon Press, 1925) p. 5.

12. *The Dramatic Works of Thomas Dekker*, ed. Fredson Bowers, 4 vols (Cambridge: Cambridge University Press, 1953–). This edition is used for all quotations from Dekker's plays and is referred to hereafter as 'Bowers'.

13. Dekker, *The Gull's Hornbook* in *The Non-Dramatic Works*, ed. A. B. Grosart (New York: Russell & Russell, 1963).

14. Ben Jonson, *Poetaster*, in *Ben Jonson*, ed. C. H. Herford and Percy Simpson, vol. IV (Oxford: Clarendon Press, 1932).

15. Thomas Heywood, *An Apology for Actors*, ed. Richard Perkinson (New York: Scholars Facsimiles, 1941) sig. H2v, sig. G.

16. Andrew Ross, *No Respect: Intellectuals and Popular Culture* (London: Routledge, 1989) p. 5.

17. On the audience see Alfred Harbage, *Shakespeare's Audience* (New York: Columbia University Press, 1941); Ann Jennalie Cook, *The Privileged Playgoers of Shakespeare's London 1576–1642* (Princeton, NJ: Princeton University Press, 1981); Martin Butler, *Theatre and Crisis 1632–1642* (London: Methuen, 1983) Appendix 1. On the connection between the audience and the subject matter of the plays see Alfred Harbage, *Shakespeare and the Rival Traditions* (Bloomington: Indiana University Press, 1952); Linda Woodbridge, *Women in the English Renaissance* (Urbana and Chicago: University of Illinois Press, 1984) p. 266. On the relationship between audience and form see Robert Weimann, *Shakespeare and the Popular Tradition in the Theatre*, ed. R. Schwartz, (Baltimore, Md.: John Hopkins University Press, 1978). The 'popularity' of Renaissance drama was most recently used as a cultural weapon in the 'Bardbiz' controversy in the *London Review of Books* over the summer of 1991. The issues are addressed by Terence Hawkes, the iniatator and one of the principle combatants, in *Meaning by Shakespeare* (London: Routledge, 1992).

18. *The Dramatic Works of Thomas Heywood*, ed. Pearson, 6 vols (New York: Russell & Russell, 1964). This edition is used for all quotations from Heywood unless otherwise indicated. It has no lineation and references are by volume number and page. Hereafter referred to as 'Pearson'.

19. Hoy, vol. I, pp. 83–4.

20. Ibid., p. 72.

21. See Bowers, vol. I, pp. 109–10.

22. W. L. Halstead, in Hoy, vol. I, p. 87.

23. Thomas Heywood, *Apology for Actors, ed. cit.*, sig. G3ᵛ.

24. Ibid., sig. B4.

25. Day had used a similar story in *The Isle of Gulls* to refer to the homosexuality of the Jacobean Court. See David Seville, 'Political Criticism and Caricature in Selected Jacobean Plays', M.Phil. thesis, University of Sheffield (1985).

26. *The Four Prentices of London* is discussed in Chapter 3.

27. See Chapter 7.

28. Gurr, *Playgoing*, p. 165.

29. See Clark, *Thomas Heywood*, p. 137; Andrew Gurr has suggested that this disparagement was a more particular rivalry between King's Men playwrights and those who, like Dekker and Heywood, wrote for Beeston's companies at the Cockpit/Phoenix in Drury Lane: 'Singing through the Chatter: Ford and Contemporary Theatrical Fashion', in Michael Neill (ed.), *John Ford Critical Revisions* (Cambridge: Cambridge University Press, 1988) pp. 81–96.

30. Brian Gibbons, *Jacobean City Comedy* (London: Methuen, 1980), quoted in Gurr, *Playgoing*, p. 155.

2　Politics and Performance

1. The debate over political readings of Renaissance drama is summarised in the introduction to the reissue of J. W. Lever, *The Tragedy of State* (Methuen: London, 1971; reissued 1987 with an introduction by Jonathan Dollimore). H. Aram Veeser, *The New Historicism* (London: Routledge, 1989) collects some key documents from the US discussion. The introduction to Richard Wilson, *Will Power* (London: Harvester, 1993) analyses the intellectual history of this movement.

2. For example, Julia Gasper, *The Dragon and the Dove* (Oxford: Oxford University Press, 1991); Margot Heinemann, 'Rebel Lords, Popular Playwrights, and Political Culture: Notes on the Jacobean Patronage of the Earl of Southampton', *Yearbook of English Studies*, vol. 21 (1991); Martin Butler, *Theatre and Crisis 1632–1642* (London: Methuen, 1984) ch. 8.

3. Heinemann, 'Rebel Lords', p. 153.

4. Thomas Heywood, *An Apology for Actors*, ed. Richard Perkinson (New York: Scholars Facsimiles, 1941) sig. E3–E3ᵛ.

5. Tilney's annotations in the MS of *The Book of Sir Thomas More*; see Antony Munday *et al.*, *The Book of Sir Thomas More*, ed. G. Gabrieli and V. Melchiori (Manchester: Manchester University Press, 1990) p. 17. All quotations from the play are taken from this edition, hereafter referred to as 'Gabrieli and Melchiori'.

6. Ibid., p. 18.

7. *Holinshed's Chronicles of England, Scotland and Ireland* (1808 edn) vol. 3, pp. 618–25.

8. For the role of women in food riots, see J. Walter, 'Grain Riots and Popular Attitudes to the Law: Maldon and the Crisis of 1629', in J.

Brewer and J. Styles (eds), *An Ungovernable People: The English and their Law in the Seventeenth and Eighteenth Centuries* (London: Hutchinson, 1980) pp. 47–84.

9. The dating and authorship problems of the play are discussed in Gabrieli and Melchiori, pp. 11–12; and in Richard Dutton, *Mastering the Revels The Regulation and Censorship of English Renaissance Drama* (London: Macmillan, 1991) pp. 81–6.

10. S. Rappaport, *Worlds within Worlds: Structures of Life in Sixteenth Century London* (Cambridge: Cambridge University Press, 1989) pp. 6–22.

11. Discussed in Hoy, vol. I, p. 312.

12. Janet Clare, *Art Made Tongue-tied by Authority: Elizabethan and Jacobean Dramatic Censorship* (Manchester: Manchester University Press, 1990) pp. 51–3.

13. Scott McMillin, *The Elizabethan Theatre and the Book of Sir Thomas More* (Ithaca, NY: Cornell University Press, 1987) p. 60.

14. Peter Lake, 'Anti-popery: The Structure of a Prejudice', in Richard Cust and Ann Hughes (eds), *Conflict in Early Stuart England: Studies in Religion and Politics 1603–1642* (London: Longmans, 1989) pp. 72–106.

15. *Foxe's Book of Martyrs*, ed. G. A. Williamson (London: Secker & Warburg, 1965) pp. 192–8.

16. Antony Fletcher, Tudor Rebellions (London: Longmans, 1973) p. 90.

17. Hoy, vol. I, pp. 331–7.

18. Fletcher, *Tudor Rebellions*, p. 81.

19. Mervyn James, 'At a Crossroads of the Political Culture: The Essex Revolt, 1601', in James (ed.), *Society, Politics and Culture: Studies in Early Modern England* (Cambridge: Cambridge University Press, 1986) pp. 416–65.

20. Ibid., p. 451.

21. *Foxe's Book of Martyrs*, pp. 433, 437, 443, 439.

22. Ibid., p. 434.

23. Ibid., p. 445.

24. The same Gresham was celebrated more fully in Part II of *If You Not Know Me You Know Nobody*. See below p. 61–6.

25. David Riggs, *Ben Jonson: A Life* (Cambridge, Mass.. Harvard University Press, 1989) p. 47.

26. Thomas Heywood, *A Funerall Elegie upon the Death of Prince Henry* (London, 1613) sig. C20^v.

27. *The Four Birds of Noahs Ark*, ed. F. P. Wilson (Oxford: Blackwell, 1924) p. 101: see also p. 42, 'A Prayer for the confusion of traytors' and pp. 53–5: 'Prayer in time of persecution'.

28. On sources of popular mythology in ballads, see Tessa Watt, *Cheap Print and Popular Piety, 1550–1640* (Cambridge: Cambridge University Press, 1991).

29. The intellectual history and representation of the trope of Truth the daughter of Time is discussed in F. Saxl, 'Veritas Filia Temporis', in

Essays Presented to Ernst Cassirer (Oxford, 1936) pp. 197–222, and in Hoy, vol. II, pp. 312–13.

30. On popular festivity associated with Elizabeth's accession day, see Frances Yates, 'Elizabethan Chivalry: The Romance of the Accession Day Tilts', *Journal of the Warburg and Courtauld Institutes*, vol. 20 (1957) 4–25

31. See Bowers, vol. II, p. 497 and note Hoy, vol. II, pp. 310–11.

3 Prentices, Citizens and the London Audience

1. See Shakespeare, *King Henry VI, Part 2*, Act IV, scenes ii, vi, vii, viii. Anon., *The Life and death of Jack Straw*, ed. K. Muir (London: Malone Society Reprints, 1957).

2. Compare Jack Cade's promise that 'There shall be in England seven halfpenny loaves sold for a penny; the three-hooped pot shall have ten hoops: and I will make it a felony to drink small beer' (*Henry VI, Part 2*, IV, ii, 60–4).

3. See Roger B. Manning, *Village Revolts: Social Protest and Popular Disturbance in England, 1509–1640* (Oxford: Clarendon Press, 1988).

4. Michael Berlin, 'Civic Ceremony in Early Modern London', *Urban History Yearbook* (1986) 15–27.

5. Ibid., p. 16.

6. See Thomas Heywood, *The Four Prentices of London*, ed. M. A. W. Gasior (London: Garland Press, 1988) pp. xlix xiv. All subsequent references are to this edition.

7. Laura Stevenson, *Praise and Paradox: Merchants and Craftsmen in Elizabethan Popular Literature* (Cambridge: Cambridge University Press, 1984).

8. Michael Berlin, 'Civic Ceremony', analyses the move from church-building to civic- and secular-building in sixteenth-century London.

9. For example, Ernest Rhys, *Thomas Dekker* (London: Unwin, n.d.) p. viii, wrote of Dekker: 'He has the rare gift of putting he, it into everything he says . . . he remains, after all has been set down, still the same lovable, elusive being, a man of genius, a child of nature.' He describes *The Shoemaker's Holiday* as 'this hearty comedy – so full of overflowing good humour . . . displays all that genial interest in everything human, all that ready democratic sympathy which, among Elizabethans, Dekker has peculiarly displayed'.

10. See Chapter 4.

11. For example, in Thomas Middleton's *Michaelmas Term* and *A Trick to Catch the Old One*.

12. Hoy, vol. III, p. 102.

13. The farcical action was the most successful part of a recent modern dress fringe production of the play and showed the durability of these fundamental comic structures. See the review in *The Times*, 25 November 1992.

14. David Bergeron, in his edition of *Thomas Heywood's Pageants*

(New York, 1986) evaluates the different pageants in terms of their dramatic coherence.

15. The political significance of this pageant is discussed in Julia Gasper, *The Dragon and the Dove* (Oxford: Oxford University Press, 1991) pp. 36–40.

16. David Riggs, *Ben Jonson: A Life* (Cambridge, Mass.: Harvard University Press, 1989) p. 11.

17. Berlin, 'Civic Ceremony', p. 20.

18. Louis B. Wright, *Middle Class Culture in Elizabethan England* (University of Carolina Press, 1935) p. 637.

4 Women and Dramatic Form

1. This was not a merely theoretical question: consider the dilemma of Justice Hales who as a staunch Protestant favoured Lady Jane Grey, but as a justice had to uphold the principle of primogeniture. See Hoy, vol. I, p. 312.

2. See Laura Mulvey, *Visual and Other Pleasures* (London: Macmillan, 1989) esp. ch. 8, 'Melodrama Inside and Outside the Home'. On women in the English history play, see Phyllis Rackin, *Stages of History* (London: Routledge, 1991) ch. 4, 'Patriarchal History and Female Subversion'.

3. Anon., *A Warning for Fair Women*, ed. C. D. Cannon (The Hague: Mouton, 1975).

4. Title page of *King Edward IV*, ed. Pearson, vol. I, p. 2.

5. Compare *Romeo and Juliet*, I, v, 45, and for a more sexualised version John Webster, *The White Devil*, I, ii, 227–8.

6. This 'looking on' scene is characteristic of Dekker and Heywood's dramatic style. Compare, for example, the scene in *The Shoemakers Holiday*, III, iv where Hammon watches Jane in her shop.

7. Thomas Heywood, *A Woman Killed with Kindness*, ed. R. W. van Fossen (London: Methuen, 1961).

8. Alan Dessen, *Elizabethan Stage Conventions and Modern Interpreters* (Cambridge: Cambridge University Press 1984) p. 111.

9. See Susan Amussen, *An Ordered Society: Gender and Class in Early Modern England* (Oxford: Blackwells, 1988); David Underdown, *Revel, Riot and Rebellion: Popular Politics and Culture in England 1603–1660* (Oxford: Clarendon Press, 1985) has described a 'crisis of order' in the relations between men and women in the period. The connection between social crisis and drama is discussed in Kathleen McLuskie, *Renaissance Dramatists* (Brighton: Harvester, 1989) ch. 2, pp. 27–56.

10. Mary Beth Rose, *The Expense of Spirit: Love and Sexuality in English Renaissance Drama* (Ithaca, NY: Cornell University Press, 1988).

11. Thomas Heywood(?), *How to Tell a Good Wife from a Bad* in *A Select Collection of Old English Plays*, ed. R. Dodsley (repr. New York: Russell & Russell, 1964).

12. See the discussion in Rose, *The Expense of Spirit*, pp. 273–4.

13. Compare the adaptation of the convention in the opening scene

of *Twelfth Night* and the association of hunting with love in *The Shoemaker's Holiday*, II, i.

14. See *Henslowe's Diary*, ed. R. A. Foakes and R. T. Rickert (Cambridge: Cambridge University Press, 1961) discussed in Hoy, vol. I, p. 130

15. Compare Shakespeare's use of this device in *All's Well that Ends Well*, II, iii, when Helena is given her choice of lords at the French court.

16. The complexities of assigning authorship to parts of the play are discussed in Hoy, vol. I, p. 146.

17. See III, ii, 59 and Hoy, vol. I, p. 165.

18. Discussed in McLuskie, *Renaissance Dramatists*, pp. 136–40.

19. Rose, *The Expense of Spirit*, pp. 13–15.

20. The story and its influence was used as a paradigm of the problems of feminist criticism by Harriet Hawkins, 'The Victim's Side: Chaucer's Clerk's Tale and Webster's *Duchess of Malfi*', *Signs*, 1 (1975) no. 2, 339–62.

5 The Challenge to the Popular Stage

1. Quoted in Clark, *Thomas Heywood*, p. 16.

2. *Pimlico or Run Redcap* (1609) sig. C; quoted in Clark, *Thomas Heywood*, p. 16

3. Francis Beaumont, *The Knight of the Burning Pestle*, in *The Dramatic Works in the Beaumont and Flecher Canon*, ed. Fredson Bowers (Cambridge: Cambridge University Press, 1966) vol. 1.

4. See, for example, Louis Wright's assertion that Elizabethan romances 'were as fascinating as the unrealities of cinema adventures are to present day shop girls', *Middle Class Culture in Elizabethan England* (University of Carolina Press, 1935) p. 322. The psychoanalytic fantasy that lies behind the association of 'low culture' with women is discussed in Jacqueline Rose, *The Haunting of Sylvia Plath* (London: Virago, 1991) ch. 2.

5. See especially the trial scene in *A Warning for Fair Women*, Act V and *A Woman Killed with Kindness*, XII, 141–4, where Anne Frankford urges women in the audience to learn from her folly.

6. See the discussion in Hoy, vol. II, pp. 160–2.

7. See above p. 86–7. The trope of the lustful tyrant was adapted in Fletcherian tragedy and tragicomedy. See Lois Potter *et al.*, *The Revels History of Drama in English*, vol. IV: *1613-1660* (London: Methuen, 1981) pp. 88–96.

8. The play was called *The Converted Courtesan* in the running titles of the original edition. See Bowers (ed.), *The Dramatic Works of Thomas Dekker*, vol. 2, p. 7. *The Conversion of an English Courtesan* is the title of a prose pamphlet by Robert Greene which works the paradigm narrative of fall, sin and conversion. See Kathleen McLuskie, 'Lawless Desires Well Tempered', in Susan Zimmerman (ed.), *Erotic Politics: Desire on the Renaissance Stage* (London: Routledge, 1992) pp. 106–7.

9. The mixture of styles and the juxtaposition of powerful local

effects was shown to have a continuing theatrical force in a recent fringe production of the play (see *The Times*, 25 November 1992). The power of its rhetoric is also evident in the passages copied by Thomas Pudsey, a member of the contemporary audience. See Hoy, vol. II, p. 67.

10. This plot is discussed in detail in Chapter 3.

11. See Simon Shepherd, *Amazons and Warrior Women: Varieties of Feminism in Seventeenth Century Drama* (Brighton: Harvester, 1981).

12. As, for example, in Shakespeare *Venus and Adonis* (229–40). The popular theatre dramatists' adaptation of cultural tropes from élite culture is evident here. Compare the love/hunt analogy noted in connection with *Patient Grissil* and *The Shoemaker's Holiday*. See Chapter 4, n. 6.

13. See Francis Lee Utley, *The Crooked Rib: An Analytical Index to the Argument about Women in English and Scots Literature to the End of the Year 1568* (New York: Octagon Books, 1970). The later debate is analysed in Linda Woodbridge, *Women in the English Renaissance* (Urbana and Chicago: University of Illinois Press, 1984).

14. As in the dance of madmen in Webster's *The Duchess of Malfi*, the madmen represent trades which feed the fashion industry and are felt to have privileged access to women.

6 The Cross-dressed Heroine

1. Michael H. Leonard, *A Critical Edition of Thomas Heywood's The Wise Woman of Hogsdon* (London: Garland, 1980).

2. Jean Howard, 'Scripts and/versus Playhouses: Ideological Production and the Renaissance Public Stage', in Valerie Wayne (ed.), *The Matter of Difference: Materialist Feminist Criticism of Shakespeare* (Hemel Hempstead: Harvester, 1991) pp. 221–36.

3. Compare the similar device in the brothel scene of *Westward Ho*; see Chapter 5.

4. *Consistory of London Correction Book*, 27 January 1611; quoted in Hoy, vol. III, pp. 1–2.

5. However, an insistence on peace and good conduct had always been a mechanism in the control of women. Petruchio in Shakespeare's *The Taming of the Shrew* triumphed that Kate's ultimate obedience would mean 'Peace . . . and love and quiet life' (V, ii, 113).

6. *Consistory of London Correction Book*, quoted in Hoy, vol. I, p. 2.

7. See Simon Shepherd, *Amazons and Warrior Women: Varieties of Feminism in Seventeenth Century Drama* (Brighton: Harvester, 1981).

8. Heywood, *An Apology for Actors*, sig. C3ᵛ. The distinction is discussed in Kathleen McLuskie, *Renaissance Dramatists* (Brighton: Harvester, 1989) pp. 101–4.

9. The pamphlet controversy over cross-dressing, *Hic Mulier: or the Man Woman* (1620) and *Haec Vir: or the Womanish Man* made clear that effeminate men were just as undesirable as mannish women. Laxton's name could punningly refer to his impotence (Lacks stones).

10. The best-known dramatic 'roaring boy' is Kastril who comes to

town to learn roaring in Ben Jonson's *The Alchemist*. Monopoly's plans to break up a whore house in *Westward Ho* would also be suitably 'roaring' behaviour. See Chapter 5.

11. The most recent of many discussions of the ideology of *The Roaring Girl* is Stephen Orgel, 'The Subtexts of *The Roaring Girl*' in Susan Zimmerman (ed.), *Erotic Politics: Desire on the Renaissance Stage* (London: Routledge, 1992) pp. 15–16.

12. *The Fair Maid of the West*, ed. Robert K. Turner (London: Edward Arnold, 1968).

13. See Louis B. Wright, *Middle Class Culture in Elizabethan England* (University of Carolina Press, 1935) p. 117.

14. Sybyl Thorndike played the witch in a Phoenix Theatre production at the Lyric Hammersmith in 1921; Edith Evans, who played Ann Ratcliffe in that production, played Elizabeth Sawyer at the Old Vic in 1936. The play was directed by Bernard Miles at the Mermaid in 1962 and by Barry Kyle with Miriam Karlin in the Royal Shakespeare Company production of 1983. See Hoy, vol. III, pp. 239–41.

15. Discussed in detail in Roger Warren 'Ford in Performance', in Michael Neill (ed.), *John Ford: Critical Revisions* (Cambridge: Cambridge University Press, 1988) pp. 24–6.

16. Keith Thomas, *Religion and the Decline of Magic:Studies in Popular Beliefs in Sixteenth and Seventeenth Century England* (Harmondsworth, Middx.: Penguin Books, 1971) and Christina Larner, *Witchcraft and Religion: The Politics of Popular Belief* (Oxford: Blackwell, 1984) analyse the particular characteristics of witchcraft in England and Scotland respectively, and suggest that levels of witchcraft accusations can be connected to different patterns of social organisation and the character of religious change.

17. Henry Goodcole, *The Wonderful Discoverie of Elizabeth Sawyer, a Witch* (London, 1621) sig. A3

18. See G. E. Bentley, 'The Theatres and the Actors', in Lois Potter *et al., The Revels of History of Drama in English*, vol. 4 (London: Methuen, 1981) pp. 91–2.

19. See Andrew Gurr, 'Singing through the Chatter: Ford and Contemporary Theatrical Fashion', in Michael Neill (ed.), *John Ford: Critical Revisions* (Cambridge: Cambridge University Press, 1988) pp. 81-96

20. Potter *et al., The Revels History of Drama in English*, p. 170.

21. Quoted in McLuskie, *Renaissance Dramatists*, pp. 74–5.

22. The phenomenon has been analysed in E. P. Thompson, 'Rough Music, Le Charivari Anglais', *Annales ESC*, vol. 27 (1972) 285–312.

23. The phenomenon of élite participation in popular culture is discussed in Barry Reay, *Popular Culture in Seventeenth Century England*, (London: Croom Helm, 1985) and David Underdown, *Revel, Riot and Rebellion: Popular Politics and Culture in England 1603–1660* (Oxford: Clarendon Press, 1985)

24. Herbert Berry, 'The Globe Bewitched and El Hombre Fiel', *Mediaeval and Renaissance Drama in England*, vol. I (1984) pp. 211–30.

25. Ibid., p. 213.
26. Ibid., p. 212.

7 The Final Years

1. See Hoy, vol. III, pp. 139–41 on the dating and causes of Dekker's imprisonment, and Clark, *Thomas Heywood*, pp. 143–86 on Heywood's non-dramatic writing.

2. Heywood's collaboration with Brome on *The Late Lancashire Witches* was produced by the Kings Men at the Globe.

3. Martin Butler, *Theatre and Crisis 1632–1642* (London: Methuen, 1984) p. 223.

4. See the preface to *A Challenge for Beauty*. The conflict between the audience and styles of Beeston's Cockpit and the King's Men's theatres is discussed in Andrew Gurr, 'Singing through the Chatter: Ford and Contemporary Theatrical Fashion', in Michael Neill (ed.), *John Ford: Critical Revisions* (Cambridge: Cambridge University Press, 1988) pp. 81–96.

5. See A. H. Gilbert, 'Thomas Heywood's Debt to Plautus', *JEGP*, vol. 12 (1913) 293–611.

6. Thomas Heywood, *The Captives or The Lost Recovered*, ed. Arthur Brown, Malone Society Reprints (Oxford: Oxford University Press, 1953). All references to the play are to this edition.

7. Ibid., ll. 192–5.

8. See Act I, iii, 562–5; the MS also indicates cuts in the bawdy at Act I, iii, 626–9.

9. Ibid., SD l. 650.

10. The use of *commedia* style scenarios by Middleton is discussed in Lois Potter *et al.*, *The Revels History of Drama in English*, vol. 4 (London: Methuen, 1981) pp. 215–18 and by Ford in Kathleen McLuskie, 'Language and Matter with a Fit of Mirth: Dramatic Construction in the plays of John Ford' in M. Neill (ed.), *John Ford Critical Revisions* (Cambridge: Cambridge University Press, 1988) pp. 97–128.

11. See Thomas Heywood, *The Captives or The Lost Recovered*, ed. Alexander Corbin Judson (New Haven, Conn.: Yale University Press, 1921) pp. 17–24.

12. The gag is used in Marlowe's *The Jew of Malta*, Act IV, i. Heywood wrote the prologue for a revival of this play at court in 1633. The same device had been used in John Heywood's interlude, *The Pardoner and the Friar*, and its continuing theatrical effectiveness was evident in a production in 1982 by the Medieval Players.

13. Compare also the brothel sequence in Fletcher's *The Humorous Leuitenant*, Act II, iii, where the bawd, Leucippe, takes a similarly opportunistic view of her victims.

14. R. M. Smuts, 'The Puritan Followers of Henrietta Maria in the 1630s', *English Historical Review* (1978) 26–45.

15. Martin Butler, 'Entertaining the Palatine Prince: Plays on Foreign Affairs 1635–1637, *ELR*, vol. 12 (1983) 319–43.

16. S. R. Gardiner (ed.), *Documents Relating to the Proceedings against William Prynne in 1634 and 1637* (London, 1877); Kim Walker, 'New Prison: Representing the Female Actor in Shirley's *The Bird in a Cage* (1633)', *ELR*, vol. 21 (1991) no. 3, 385–400.

17. See Clark, *Thomas Heywood*, p. 140.

18. Ibid., p. 142.

19. Walker, 'New Prison', p. 393.

20. The same motif of the contest between Apollo and Pan was used to discuss the conflict between élite and mass culture by Tony Harrison in *The Trackers of Oxyrhyncus* in 1991. For Harrison, the triumph of Apollo and the flaying of Marsyas which ensued, closed the possibility of a unified culture shared by all people and left popular culture to become debased and alienated by commerce.

21. Compare the scene in Vulcan's smithy in Dekker's *London's Tempe* in honour of the Ironmongers.

22. See Raymond C. Shady, 'Thomas Heywood's Masque at Court', in G. R. Hibbard (ed.), *The Elizabethan Theatre*, vol. 7 (London: Macmillan, 1981) pp. 117–66.

23. Hoy, vol. III, p. 144

24. Potter *et al.*, *The Revels History of Drama in English*, pp 188–94.

25. Jerzy Limon, *Dangerous Matter: English Drama and Politics in 1623/4* (Cambridge: Cambridge University Press, 1986) pp. 96–7; Julia Gasper, *The Dragon and the Dove* (Oxford: Oxford University Press, 1991) pp. 192–6; G. E. Bentley, *The Jacobean and Caroline Stage* (Oxford: Clarendon Press, 1956) p. 461.

Bibliography

Susan Amussen, *An Ordered Society: Gender and Class in Early Modern England* (Oxford: Blackwell, 1988).

Anon., *The Life and Death of Jack Straw*, ed. K. Muir (London: Malone Society, 1957).

Anon., *A Warning for Fair Women*, ed. C. D. Cannon (The Hague: Mouton, 1975).

Francis Beaumont, *The Knight of the Burning Pestle* in *The Dramatic Works in the Beaumont and Fletcher Canon*, ed. Fredson Bowers (Cambridge: Cambridge University Press, 1966) vol. 1.

G. E. Bentley, *The Profession of Dramatist in Shakespeare's Time, 1590–1642* (Princeton, NJ: Princeton University Press, 1971).

G. E. Bentley, *The Jacobean and Caroline Stage* (Oxford: Clarendon Press, 1956) 6 vols.

David Bergeron, 'The Patronage of Dramatists: The Case of Thomas Heywood', *English Literary Renaissance*, vol. 18 (1988) 294–305.

David Bergeron (ed.), *Thomas Heywood's Pageants: A Critical Edition* (New York: 1986).

Michael Berlin, 'Civic Ceremony in Early Modern London', *Urban History Yearbook* (1986) 15–27.

Herbert Berry, 'The Globe Bewitched and El Hombre Fiel', *Mediaeval and Renaissance Drama in England*, vol. 1 (1984) 211–30.

Martin Butler, 'Entertaining the Palatine Prince: Plays on Foreign Affairs 1635–1637', *ELR*, vol. 12 (1983) 319–43.

Martin Butler, *Theatre and Crisis 1632–1642* (London: Methuen, 1984).

Neil Carson, *A Companion to Henslowe's Diary* (Cambridge: Cambridge University Press, 1988).

Janet Clare, *Art Made Tongue-tied by Authority: Elizabethan and Jacobean Dramatic Censorship* (Manchester: Manchester University Press, 1989).

A. M. Clark, *Thomas Heywood, Playwright and Miscellanist* (New York: Russell & Russell, 1958).

Ann Jennalie Cook, *The Privileged Playgoers of Shakespeare's London 1576–1642* (Princeton, NJ: Princeton University Press, 1981).

Thomas Dekker, *The Dramatic Works of Thomas Dekker*, ed. Fredson Bowers (Cambridge: Cambridge University Press, 1953) 4 vols.

Thomas Dekker, *The Four Birds of Noah's Ark*, ed. F. P. Wilson (Oxford: Blackwell, 1924).

Thomas Dekker, *The Gull's Hornbook*, in *The Non-Dramatic Works*, ed. A. B. Grosart (New York: Russell & Russell, 1963).

Alan Dessen, *Elizabethan Stage Conventions and Modern Interpreters* (Cambridge: Cambridge University Press, 1984).

Richard Dutton, *Mastering the Revels, The Regulation and Censorship of English Renaissance Drama* (London: Macmillan, 1991) pp. 81–6.

C. R. Forker and J. Candido, 'Wit, Wisdom and Theatricality in *The Book of Sir Thomas More*', *Shakespeare Studies*, vol. 13 (1980) 85–104.

Antony Fletcher, *Tudor Rebellions*, (London: Longman, 1973)

S. R. Gardiner (ed.), *Documents Relating to the Proceedings against William Prynne in 1634 and 1637* (London, 1877).

Julia Gasper, *The Dragon and the Dove* (Oxford: Oxford University Press, 1991).

Brian Gibbons, *Jacobean City Comedy* (London: Methuen, 1980).

A. H. Gilbert, 'Thomas Heywood's Debt to Plautus', *JEGP*, vol. 12 (1913) 293–611.

Henry Goodcole, *The Wonderful Discoverie of Elizabeth Sawyer, a Witch* (London, 1621).

Robert Greene, *The Conversion of an English Courtesan*, in F. Aydelotte (ed.), *Elizabethan Rogues and Vagabondes* (Oxford: Clarendon Press, 1913).

Andrew Gurr, *Playgoing in Shakespeare's London* (Cambridge: Cambridge University Press, 1987).

Andrew Gurr, 'Singing through the Chatter: Ford and Contemporary Theatrical Fashion', in Michael Neill (ed.), *John Ford Critical Revisions* (Cambridge: Cambridge University Press, 1988) pp. 81–96.

Alfred Harbage, *Shakespeare's Audience* (New York: Columbia University Press, 1941).

Alfred Harbage, *Shakespeare and the Rival Traditions* (Bloomington: Indiana University Press, 1952).

Terence Hawkes, *Meaning by Shakespeare* (London: Routledge, 1992).

Harriet Hawkins, 'The Victim's Side: Chaucer's Clerk's Tale and Webster's *The Duchess of Malfi*', *Signs*, vol. 1 (1975) no. 2, 339–62.

William Hazlitt (ed.), *A Select Collection of Old English Plays . . . Originally published by Robert Dodsley* (London 1874–6; reprinted New York: Russell & Russell, 1964).

Henslowe's Diary, ed. R. A. Foakes and F. T. Rickert (Cambridge: Cambridge University Press, 1961).

Thomas Heywood, *An Apology for Actors*, ed. Richard Perkinson (New York: Scholars Facsimiles, 1941).

Thomas Heywood, *The Captives or The Lost Recovered*, ed. Arthur Brown, Malone Society Reprints (Oxford: Oxford University Press, 1953).

Thomas Heywood, *The Captives or The Lost Recovered*, ed. Alexander Corbin Judson (New Haven, Conn.: Yale University Press, 1921).

Thomas Heywood, *A Critical Edition of Thomas Heywood's The Wise Woman of Hogsdon*, ed. Michael H. Leonard (London: Garland, 1980).

Thomas Heywood, *The Four Prentices of London*, ed. M. A. Gasior (London: Garland 1988).

Thomas Heywood, *A Funerall Elegie upon the Death of Prince Henrie* (London, 1613).

Thomas Heywood, *The Dramatic Works of Thomas Heywood*, ed. Pearson (New York: Russell & Russell, 1964).

Thomas Heywood, *A Woman Killed with Kindness*, ed. R. W. van Fossen (London: Methuen, 1961).

Thomas Heywood, *The Fair Maid of the West*, ed. Robert K. Turner, (London: Edward Arnold, 1968).

Margot Heinemann, 'Rebel Lords, Popular Playwrights, and Political Culture: Notes on the Jacobean Patronage of the Earl of Southampton', *Yearbook of English Studies*, vol. 21 (1991) 63–86.

Holinshed's Chronicles of England, Scotland and Ireland, vol. 3 (1808) pp. 618–25.

Jean Howard, 'Scripts and/versus Playhouses: Ideological Production and the Renaissance Public Stage', in Valerie Wayne (ed.), *The Matter of Difference. Materialist Feminist Criticism of Shakespeare* (London: Harvester, 1991) pp. 221–36.

Cyrus Hoy, *Introduction, Notes and Commentaries to Texts in The Dramatic Works of Thomas Dekker*, 4 vols (Cambridge: Cambridge University Press, 1980).

Mervyn James, 'At the Crossroads of the Political Culture: the Essex Revolt, 1601', in James (ed.), *Society, Politics and Culture: Studies in Early Modern England* (Cambridge: Cambridge University Press, 1986) pp. 416–65.

Roslyn Knutson, 'Henslowe's Diary and the Economics of Play Revision for Revival 1592–1603', *Theatre Research International*, vol. 10 (1985) 1–18.

Peter Lake, 'Anti-popery: the Structure of a Prejudice' in Richard Cust and Ann Hughes (eds.), *Conflict in Early Stuart England: Studies in Religion and Politics 1603–1642* (London: Longman, 1989) pp. 72–106.

Charles Lamb, *Specimens of the English Dramatic Poets who Lived About the Time of Shakespeare* (London: Dutton, 1887).

Christina Larner, *Witchcraft and Religion: The Politics of Popular Belief* (Oxford: Blackwell, 1984).

J. W. Lever, *The Tragedy of State* (Methuen: London, 1971). Reissued 1987 with an introduction by Jonathan Dollimore.

Jerzy Limon, *Dangerous Matter: English Drama and Politics in 1623/4*, (Cambridge: Cambridge University Press, 1986).

Roger B. Manning, *Village Revolts: Social Protest and Popular Disturbance in England 1509–1640* (Oxford: Clarendon Press, 1988).

Kathleen McLuskie, *Renaissance Dramatists* (Brighton: Harvester, 1989).

Kathleen McLuskie, 'The Poets Royal Exchange: Patronage and

Commerce in Early Modern Drama', *Yearbook of English Studies*, vol. 21 (1991) 53–62.

Kathleen McLuskie, 'Lawless Desires Well Tempered', in Susan Zimmerman (ed.), *Erotic Politics*, pp. 103–26.

Scott McMillin, 'The Book of Sir Thomas More: A Theatrical View', *Modern Philology*, vol. 68 (1970), 10–24.

Scott McMillin, *The Elizabethan Theatre and the Book of Sir Thomas More* (Ithaca, NY: Cornell University Press, 1987).

Laura Mulvey, *Visual and Other Pleasures* (London: Macmillan, 1989).

Antony Munday *et al.*, *The Book of Sir Thomas More*, ed. V. Gabrieli and G. Melchiori (Manchester: Manchester University Press, 1990).

Michael Neill (ed.), *John Ford Critical Revisions* (Cambridge: Cambridge University Press, 1988).

Stephen Orgel, 'The Subtexts of *The Roaring Girl*', in Susan Zimmerman, *Erotic Politics*, pp. 12–26.

Lois Potter *et al.*, *The Revels History of Drama in English*, vol. 4: *1613–1660* (London: Methuen, 1981).

Phyllis Rackin, *Stages of History* (London: Routledge, 1991).

S. Rappaport, *Worlds Within Worlds: Structures of Life in Sixteenth Century London* (Cambridge: Cambridge University Press, 1989).

Barry Reay, *Popular Culture in Seventeenth Century England* (London: Croom Helm, 1985).

David Riggs, *Ben Jonson: A Life* (Cambridge, Mass: Harvard University Press, 1990).

Jacqueline Rose, *The Haunting of Sylvia Plath* (London: Virago, 1991).

Mary Beth Rose, *The Expense of Spirit: Love and Sexuality in English Renaissance Drama* (Ithaca, NY: Cornell University Press, 1988).

Andrew Ross, *No Respect: Intellectuals and Popular Culture* (London: Routledge, 1989).

David Seville, 'Political Criticism and Caricature in Selected Jacobean Plays', M.Phil. thesis, University of Sheffield (1985).

Raymond C. Shady, 'Thomas Heywood's Masque at Court' in G. R. Hibbard (ed.), *The Elizabethan Theatre*, vol. 7 (London: Macmillan, 1981) pp. 117–66.

J. Sharpe, '"Last Dying Speeches": Religion, Ideology and Public Execution in Seventeenth Century England', *Past and Present*, vol. 107 (1985) 144–167.

Simon Shepherd, *Amazons and Warrior Women: Varieties of Feminism in Seventeenth Century Drama* (Brighton: Harvester, 1981).

Rosco Small, *The Stage Quarell between Jonson and the so called Poetasters*, (Breslau, 1899).

R. M. Smuts, 'The Puritan Followers of Henrietta Maria in the 1630s', *English Historical Review* (1978) 26–45.

Laura Stevenson, *Praise and Paradox: Merchants and Craftsmen in Elizabethan Popular Literature* (Cambridge: Cambridge University Press, 1984).

Gary Taylor, *Reinventing Shakespeare: A Cultural History from the Restoration to the Present* (London: Chatto, 1990).

Keith Thomas, *Religion and the Decline of Magic: Studies in Popular Beliefs in Sixteenth and Seventeenth Century England* (Harmondsworth, Middx.: Penguin Books, 1971).

E. P. Thompson, 'Rough Music, Le Charivari Anglais', *Annales ESC*, vol. 27 (1972) 285–312.

David Underdown, *Revel, Riot and Rebellion: Popular Politics and Culture in England 1603–1660* (Oxford: Clarendon Press, 1985).

H. Aram Veeser, *The New Historicism* (London: Routledge, 1989).

Kim Walker, 'New Prison: Representing the Female Actor in Shirley's *The Bird in a Cage* (1633)', *ELR*, vol. 21 (1991) 385–400.

J. Walter, 'Grain Riots and Popular Attitudes to the Law: Maldon and the Crisis of 1629', in J. Brewer and J. Styles (eds), *An Ungovernable People: The English and their Law in the Seventeenth and Eighteenth Centuries* (London: Hutchinson, 1980) pp. 47–84

Roger Warren, 'Ford in Performance' in Neill, *John Ford Critical Revisions*, pp. 24–6.

Tessa Watt, *Cheap Print and Popular Piety, 1550–1640* (Cambridge: Cambridge University Press, 1991).

John Webster, *The White Devil*, ed. John Russell Brown (London: Methuen, 1960).

Robert Weimann, *Shakespeare and the Popular Tradition in the Theatre*, ed. R. Schwartz (Baltimore, Md.: Johns Hopkins University Press, 1978).

Linda Woodbridge, *Women in the English Renaissance* (Urbana and Chicago: University of Illinois Press, 1984).

G. E. Williamson (ed.), *Foxe's Book of Martyrs* (Secker & Warburg: London, 1965).

Louis B. Wright, *Middle Class Culture in Elizabethan England* (State University of Carolina Press, 1935).

Frances Yates, 'Elizabethan Chivalry: The Romance of the Accession Day Tilts', *Journal of the Warburg and Courtauld Institutes*, vol. 20 (1957) 4–25.

Susan Zimmerman (ed.), *Erotic Politics: Desire on the Renaissance Stage* (London: Routledge, 1992).

Index